Healthcare Documentation

Career
Step

Career Step, LLC
Phone: 801.489.9393
Toll-Free: 800.246.7837
Fax: 801.491.6645
careerstep.com

This text companion contains a snapshot of the online program content converted to a printed format. Please note that the online training program is constantly changing and improving and is always the source of the most up-to-date information.

Product Number: HG-PR-11-007
Generation Date: February 2, 2012

Table of Contents

Unit 1
Introduction

Introduction to Healthcare Documentation

Learning Objective

This module provides the student with an overview of healthcare documentation, including documentation types, report components, and formatting. The student will become familiar with healthcare documentation standards, HIPAA compliance regulations, and the adaptation of the electronic health record (EHR) in institutions throughout the United States and the world. Upon completion, the student will understand the role of the medical transcription editor in maintaining the integrity and confidentiality of the medical record.

The Healthcare Documentation module focuses on the patient's medical record. Specifically, this module will help you understand the medical record better—where it comes from, what it contains, and how the integrity and the confidentiality of the medical record information in it is protected.

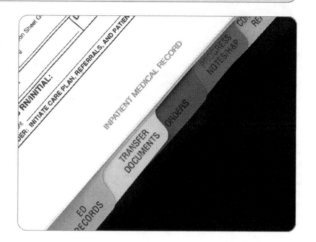

Unit 2
Documentation Basics

Documentation Basics – Introduction

We talked about the medical record in the Introduction (but that was before all the technical gobbledygook from Technology and the Medical Professional module). Let's quickly review the healthcare documentation process.

Healthcare documentation process:

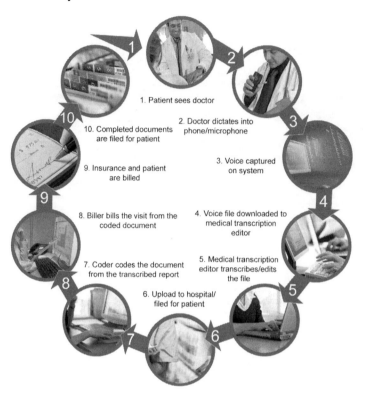

1. Patient sees doctor

2. Doctor dictates into phone/microphone

3. Voice captured on system

4. Voice file downloaded to medical transcription editor

5. Medical transcription editor transcribes/edits the file

6. Upload to hospital/filed for patient

7. Coder codes the document from the transcribed report

8. Biller bills the visit from the coded document

9. Insurance and patient are billed

10. Completed documents are filed for patient

Remember this graphic? We discussed how the **healthcare documentation process** is the process by which the **medical record** containing the details of a patient's healthcare visit(s) is created and stored. The patient provides personal and health information at the beginning of a visit and throughout the healthcare documentation process. This helps the doctor dictate the information correctly for the transcriptionist, the coders and billers, and finally for insurance purposes. In other instances, speech recognition software translates the doctors' dictations, in which case a medical transcription editor would edit the data.

Patient Information

The critical element to be added to complete the healthcare documentation process is **patient information**. Patient information includes facts about the patient (also known as **patient demographics**), as well as personal and medical information, such as his/her living situation, **symptom** (a change in health function experienced by a patient), symptom onset, personal and medical history, family history, and other relevant information. The patient's personal information can be obtained verbally, in writing, or using a combination of both.

Demographic and personal information, reason for admission, and usually some patient-supplied information form the foundation for the medical record. By the time the doctor or healthcare worker providing treatment sees the patient, the process of gathering information has already begun!

The process of gathering this information actually begins when the appointment is made. The scheduling secretary should ask (and make note of) the primary reason for requesting the appointment. If the patient is a new patient, demographic and medical information is collected through a form or series of forms as soon as the patient appears at the front desk.

The forms are not just designed to give the patient writer's cramps (although that can be a side effect), but to obtain information from the patient that is both accurate and complete. This information is vital in evaluating patient complaints and providing treatment. Personal information is also extremely important in processing medical claims and submitting bills.

Let's delve a little deeper into patient demographics and patient-provided information collected for the medical record.

I. **TRUE/FALSE.**
   Mark the following true or false.

   1. Patient demographics are basic facts about the patient.

      ○ true
      ○ false

   2. The patient's demographics and personal information can only be obtained in writing.

      ○ true
      ○ false

3. The foundation of the medical record is formed only of demographic information.
   ○ true
   ○ false

4. The process of gathering patient information begins when the appointment is made.
   ○ true
   ○ false

Patient Demographics

At some point in the process, virtually every healthcare worker is involved in gathering patient information. As noted earlier, the receptionist (or medical secretary) makes the first entries into the patient's medical record by collecting **patient demographics** when the patient arrives for an appointment. Demographics include basic information such as name, address, telephone number, gender, date of birth, and insurance/billing information. This information is important, and it is updated and verified as necessary throughout patient care and the healthcare documentation process. Weeks or months after the initial visit, medical billing specialists or office staff may contact the patient to ask for additional or corrected demographic information.

Patient information—age, gender, insurance, medical history—is an important factor for establishing and managing healthcare.

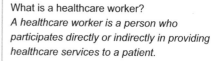

Highlights

What is a healthcare worker?
A healthcare worker is a person who participates directly or indirectly in providing healthcare services to a patient.

A healthcare worker can be a: doctor, medical secretary, nurse, physician's assistant, nurse's aide, admissions clerk, laboratory or radiology technician, and many others.

Collection of Patient Information

Once basic patient demographics are collected, the process of gathering more detailed health and personal information comes next. The patient provides the first information by completing a form or forms such as the one below.

We've placed a multi-page visual aid in the appendix on pages 160-162.

Not all healthcare providers will gather this information by having the patient fill out forms. For example, for most emergency room visits, an admitting or evaluating nurse (**triage nurse**) conducts a brief interview with the patient or patient's family member and documents the patient's reason for admission—symptoms, brief history, etc. This is also the point at which **vital signs**—height, weight, temperature, respiratory rate, pulse, and blood pressure—are performed and recorded.

Except in extreme medical emergencies, patient information is collected and reviewed prior to patient examination and treatment. Even during emergencies, every attempt is made to obtain pertinent patient history and details of any specific injuries or ongoing medical problem from the patient, witnesses, and/or family members. This information can be a matter of life or death in providing appropriate treatment and medication.

We've now arrived back to step #1 in the healthcare documentation process and the medical record is handed to the healthcare provider actually providing treatment to the patient. Only now, the medical record contains enough information for the doctor to know who the patient is and why he/she is seeking treatment.

Subjective/Objective Data

Once the patient has provided basic information, healthcare personnel begin collecting and recording more detailed and pertinent information. The treating nurse, physician, or other provider will ask the patient more detailed questions and record the answers, as well as make observations about the way the patient looks, acts, interacts, and appears on physical examination.

You probably noticed that a couple of different methods have been described for obtaining patient information—one involves asking questions, obtaining descriptions, and interviewing and filling out forms. The other involves observing, examining, and recording results. These are commonly known as **subjective** and **objective**.

Subjective means dependent on the mind or on an individual's perception for its existence.

Objective means factual or not influenced by personal feelings or opinions.

In simpler terms, subjective information is the information provided by a patient or patient's family describing how he/she feels, what happened, where it hurts, or what's causing the problem.

> **Subjective examples:**
>
> "I fell and hit my head. The top of my head hurts when I touch it."
> "I'm running a fever. I feel hot and flushed."

Objective information is the data collected from observation and examination—measuring, looking, touching, or testing.

> **Objective examples:**
>
> Head exam: The patient has a 2-inch cut on the top of the head.
> Temperature: 100.1 degrees F

All of the information—demographics, patient-supplied information, subjective/objective statements, and results recorded—is compiled into a medical record. As you can imagine, the medical record is filled with personal, sensitive information and is getting larger each minute. The rest of this module focuses on the importance of accurate documentation, confidentiality, ethical issues, privacy laws, and what is known as electronic health records.

Let's take a few minutes to review the concepts we've covered so far, and then we'll move on!

Collecting Patient Information

Have you ever taken a child to an urgent care clinic for an ear infection or other condition? You probably noticed that a day or two after treatment, a nurse or other provider called to see how the child is doing. Is the antibiotic working? Is he still having pain? This is an example of patient information being collected in the period following treatment.

Have you ever phoned in to "pre-register" for a lab or x-ray test or a same-day surgery? Registration staff ask you for personal data to begin your medical record and give you pre-surgery or pre-test information prior to your arrival at the hospital. This is patient information collected prior to (sometimes up to two weeks in advance) admission for treatment!

I. MULTIPLE CHOICE.
Choose whether the following example is subjective or objective.

1. Patient feels nauseated and has feelings of disorientation.

   ○ subjective
   ○ objective

2. Patient has a temperature of 101.2 degrees F.

   ○ subjective
   ○ objective

3. Patient has a burst left eardrum.

   ○ subjective
   ○ objective

4. Patient feels pain in their left ear.

   ○ subjective
   ○ objective

Unit 3
Documentation Standards

Documentation Standards – Introduction

The importance of accurate and timely medical record documentation and protecting the confidentiality of the medical record cannot be overemphasized. Why not? Because behind every medical record there is a person—a real person. Here are a few scenarios to bring home the importance of accuracy, timeliness, and confidentiality.

Behind every medical record there is a person—a real person.

Scenario 1:

You are scheduled to undergo a surgical procedure on your left leg. The documentation in your medical record inaccurately states the surgery is to be performed on your right leg. You are taken to the operating room where they operate on the wrong leg.

Scenario 2:

Your daughter is brought to the emergency room following an accident and is admitted to the hospital. A history is taken, including the fact that she is allergic to penicillin, but the report is not returned to the medical record for several days. Your daughter develops a dangerously high fever and is given a shot of penicillin. She goes into anaphylactic shock and comes close to death.

Scenario 3:

Kelly visits a local clinic for blood work and learns she has AIDS. The clinic's computer is "hacked" into and her personal information and AIDS status are printed on an anti-homosexual flyer in her hometown.

Scenario 4:

Your husband suffers from depression. He is treated with medication and counseling and copes well with family and work. He applies for a promotion but is denied because his boss heard from his neighbor, a nurse at your husband's clinic, about his depression and thinks it might affect his ability to do a good job.

Each of these scenarios represents a serious breakdown in the handling of private healthcare information. As you can see, the consequences can be embarrassing, painful, and—at worst—catastrophic. Quality documentation is an important component of quality patient care. In the next lessons, we'll take a closer look at (1) organizations that provide medical records documentation standards and oversight, (2) medical records documentation standards, (3) common documentation errors, and (4) the role medical transcription editors play in ensuring integrity in the medical record.

Healthcare Documentation Organizations

The United States has progressed from the days of the wild, wild West when the storekeeper could hang out a shingle in a one-horse town and say he sold chocolate bars and tobacco, cut hair, extracted teeth, and removed bullets! Today, if you want to hang out a "shingle" as a healthcare provider, your rights and responsibilities are clear. Healthcare services are regulated and can only be provided by professionals under strict state and federal guidelines. Standards for healthcare documentation are laid out by accrediting organizations and monitored by governmental and accrediting organization oversight.

Accredit - to endorse or approve officially

In the United States, medical record documentation must be uniform, accurate, complete, legible, and timely. It is the responsibility of every healthcare professional (also known as **HIM [health information management] professional**) to be informed about healthcare documentation standards and to work with other HIM professionals to ensure accurate, timely documentation so that patients receive quality care.

Several organizations have developed medical record documentation standards. One such organization is The Joint Commission. This organization accredits the majority of U.S. hospitals and other healthcare organizations. In addition to The Joint Commission, here is a partial list of organizations that have established documentation standards:

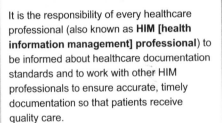

Highlights

It is the responsibility of every healthcare professional (also known as **HIM [health information management] professional**) to be informed about healthcare documentation standards and to work with other HIM professionals to ensure accurate, timely documentation so that patients receive quality care.

- National Committee for Quality Assurance (NCQA)
- American Accreditation Healthcare Commission/Utilization Review Accreditation Commission (AAHCC/URAC)
- American Osteopathic Association (AOA)
- Commission on Accreditation of Rehabilitation Facilities (CARF)
- Health Accreditation Program of the National League of Nursing
- College of American Pathologists (CAP)
- American Association of Blood Banks (AABB)
- American College of Surgeons (ACS)
- Accreditation Association for Ambulatory Healthcare (AAAHC)
- American Medical Accreditation Program (AMAP)
- American Health Information Management Association (AHIMA)

Depending on where your career path takes you and what type of healthcare provider employs you, you will be involved with one or more of these organizations. It is essential that health information management (HIM) professionals become familiar with the standards and documentation requirements of the organizations which provide oversight to their employer. Documentation standards change from year to year. Medical transcription editors (and all HIM professionals) need to stay abreast of updates and changes so they can assure ongoing quality patient care.

You don't need to memorize all of these organizations, but it's a good idea to recognize them and be familiar with their names.

I. FILL IN THE BLANK.

In the box below, find the healthcare organization that corresponds to each acronym and enter the name of the organization in the blank.

1. ACS _____

2. URAC _____

3. AHIMA _____

4. CAP _____

5. AAAHC _____

6. NCQA _____

7. CARF _____

8. AMAP _____

9. AOA _____

10. AAHCC _____

National Committee for Quality Assurance
American Accreditation Healthcare Commission
Utilization Review Accreditation Commission
American Osteopathic Association
Accreditation Association for Ambulatory Healthcare
American College of Surgeons
College of American Pathologists
American Medical Accreditation Program
American Health Information Management Association
Commission on Accreditation of Rehabilitation Facilities

Documentation Standards

Documentation standards are developed by different organizations to ensure the uniformity, accuracy, completeness, legibility, authenticity, frequency, and format of medical record entries.

As mentioned above, many organizations provide **documentation standards** and oversight. The American Health Information Management Association (AHIMA) has developed general documentation standards/guidelines to ensure patients receive quality care. We'll use the AHIMA standards as an example.

Highlights

Documentation standards are developed by different organizations to ensure the uniformity, accuracy, completeness, legibility, authenticity, frequency, and format of medical record entries.

The guidelines developed by AHIMA include the following:

Standard 1: Every healthcare organization should have policies that ensure the uniformity of both the content and the format of the medical record. The policies should be based on all applicable accreditation standards, federal and state regulations, payer requirements, and professional practice standards.

Standard 2: The medical record should be organized systematically in order to facilitate data retrieval and compilation.

Standard 3: Only individuals authorized by the organization's policies should be allowed to enter documentation in the medical record.

Standard 4: Organizational policy and/or the medical staff rules and regulations should specify who may receive and transcribe or edit verbal physician's orders.

Standard 5: Medical record entries should be documented at the time that the services they describe are rendered.

Standard 6: The authors of all entries should be clearly identified in the record.

Standard 7: Only abbreviations and symbols approved by the organization and/or medical staff rules and regulations should be used in the medical record.

Standard 8: All entries in the medical record should be permanent.

Standard 9: Errors in paper-based records should be corrected according to the following process: Draw a single line in ink through the incorrect entry. Then print the word error at the top of the entry along with a legal signature or initials and the date, time, and reason for change and the title and discipline of the individual making the correction. The correct information is then added to the entry. Errors may never be obliterated. The original entry should remain legible, and the corrections should be entered in chronological order. Any late entries should be labeled as such. Similar requirements apply to computer-based records.

Standard 10: Any corrections or information added to the record by the patient should be inserted as an addendum. No changes should be made in the original entries in the record. Any information added to the medical record by the patient should be clearly identified as an addendum.

Standard 11: The health information department (medical records) should develop, implement, and evaluate policies and procedures related to the qualitative and quantitative analysis of medical records.

Documentation (a medical record) that conforms to documentation standards—presenting an accurate, complete, legible, chronological account of the care provided to the patient—is known as **acceptable documentation.**

Documentation which does not conform to documentation standards—unclear, incomplete, or inaccurate–is known as **unacceptable documentation.**

> **Highlights**
>
> **Definition:**
> **Qualitative analysis:** Review of the medical record to ensure that standards are met and to determine accuracy of record documentation.
> **Quantitative analysis:** Review of the medical record to determine its completeness.

> **Acceptable documentation** – Documentation (a medical record) that conforms to documentation standards—presenting an accurate, complete, legible, chronological account of the care provided to the patient.

> **Unacceptable documentation** – Documentation that does not conform to documentation standards—is unclear, incomplete, or inaccurate.

Consistency

Let's look at a couple more points on the general documentation standards. The first relates to the first standard, "…the uniformity of both the content and the format of the medical record." In health information management, "uniformity of content" does not mean every patient has to get sick with the same thing! **Uniformity of content or vocabulary standards** means that common definitions of medical terms that encourage consistent descriptions of a patient's condition in the medical record are used. Still clear as mud? What does that mean? In simple terms, it means healthcare documentation should use the common and acceptable medical terms for describing patient conditions and treatments. Slang terms, ambiguous, uncommon, or unusual terms should be avoided, and consistent, clear language should be used within a report to describe a patient's condition and treatment.

The second of the "couple more points" relates to standard #11, ".... develop, implement, and evaluate policies and procedures related to the qualitative and quantitative analysis of medical records." This is a check, check, and double check principle. Medical records should be reviewed while they are being created, compiled and upon completion. Medical records documentation audits of individual records and provider records should be done consistently.

We threw a couple of definitions onto the standards page for qualitative analysis and quantitative analysis. Go back a page or two before the last exercise and see if you can find them.

Now, which definition is qualitative analysis and which definition is quantitative analysis?

Challenge Box

1. DEFINITION 1: Review of the medical record to ensure that standards are met and to determine accuracy of record documentation.
2. DEFINITION 2: Review of the medical record to determine its completeness.

Types of Audits

There are three other types of reviews or audits you should be aware of:

Review or Audit	Meaning
Concurrent review	Review of the medical record carried out while the patient is actively receiving care.
Occurrence screening	Review technique of medical records of current and discharged patients with the goal of identifying events which could potentially lead to compensation by the healthcare provider.
Retrospective review	Review of the medical record after the patient has been discharged.

Concurrent reviews are conducted while the patient is receiving treatment. HIM professionals and document authors review the records as they are created and compiled. The benefit of this type of review is that documentation issues can be identified at the time of patient care and rectified (if necessary) in a timely manner.

Occurrence screening is a **risk management-related** audit. The reviewer looks for accidents, omissions, or medical errors which resulted or could potentially result in a personal injury or loss of property. Occurrences include instances when the wrong surgery was performed or an informed consent for a procedure was not obtained. (We'll talk more about risk management in the next lesson.)

Retrospective review does not allow for timely identification of documentation issues but is still very useful for identifying and addressing weaknesses in documentation processes, areas where staff need additional training, and, where appropriate, addressing deficiencies in individual records.

It's time for some review and practice. We've covered a lot of ground. Tune in after the exercise break and we'll talk about risk management and common documentation errors.

Review: Consistency and Auditing

The following are common terms related to medical record documentation.

I. TERMINOLOGY.
Enter each term in the space provided. Read the definition and description for each term.

1. **acceptable documentation** _____

Complete, legible, and chronological account of the care provided to the patient as represented in the medical record.

2. **concurrent review** _____

Review of the medical record done while the patient is in the hospital. The benefits of this type of review are that documentation issues can be identified at the time of patient care and rectified in a timely manner.

3. **documentation standards** _____

Standards developed by different organizations (for example, The Joint Commission) to ensure the uniformity, accuracy, completeness, legibility, authenticity, timeliness, frequency, and format of medical record entries.

4. **The Joint Commission** _____

Organization which accredits hospitals and other healthcare organizations based on accreditation standards, including documentation standards.

5. **occurrence screening** _____

Technique in which the medical record of current and discharged patients is reviewed with the goal of identifying potential compensable events (accident or medical error which results in a personal injury or loss of property). Occurrences include instances when a wrong surgery was performed or an informed consent for a procedure was not obtained.

6. **qualitative analysis** _____

Review of the medical record to ensure that standards are met and to determine the accuracy of documentation.

7. **quantitative analysis** _____

Review of the medical record to determine its completeness.

8. **retrospective review** _____

Review of the medical record after the patient has been discharged. This type of review does not allow for timely identification of documentation issues.

9. **risk management** _____

Medical, legal, and administrative operations within a healthcare organization to minimize the exposure to liability. Complete and accurate medical record documentation is the foundation for effective risk management.

10. **unacceptable documentation** _____

Unclear or incomplete medical record documentation. For example, inconsistent entries.

11. **vocabulary standards** _____

Common definitions of medical terms which encourage consistent descriptions of a patient's conditions in the medical record.

II. **MATCHING.**
   Match the term and the definition. Enter the letter for the corresponding definition next to the term.

1. ____ concurrent review

2. ____ documentation standards

3. ____ acceptable documentation

4. ____ qualitative analysis

5. ____ The Joint Commission

6. ____ occurrence screening

7. ____ unacceptable documentation

8. ____ retrospective review

9. ____ vocabulary standards

10. ____ quantitative analysis

A. Complete, legible, and chronological account of patient care.

B. Incomplete or unclear information in a medical record.

C. Organization which accredits hospitals based on accreditation standards.

D. Medical record review performed after the patient has been discharged.

E. Review of the medical record to identify potential medical errors.

F. Common definitions of medical terms in the patient's medical record.

G. Review of the medical record while the patient is still a patient.

H. Developed to ensure the uniformity, accuracy, and completeness of medical record entries.

I. Review of medical record to ensure that documentation standards are met.

J. Medical record review for completeness.

III. FILL IN THE BLANK.
Select the word or phrase from the box which best completes the sentence. Complete the sentence by entering the selected word or phrase in the blank provided.

1. _____ were developed to ensure medical record entries are accurate, complete, and legible.

2. Complete, legible, and chronological account of the patient's care is referred to as _____.

3. A(n) _____ can identify documentation issues (which can be rectified in a timely manner) while the patient is in the hospital.

4. A(n) _____ is the review of the medical record to identify potential medical errors.

5. A(n) _____ is performed to ensure the accuracy of documentation in the medical record.

6. A(n) _____ is used to determine the completeness of the medical record.

7. Information in the medical record which is unclear or incomplete is called _____.

8. A(n) _____ does not allow for timely identification of documentation problems but is useful for identifying trends and areas where improvements are needed.

concurrent review
documentation standards
unacceptable documentation
retrospective review
qualitative analysis
acceptable documentation
occurrence screening
quantitative analysis

Risk Management

Need a break? We've covered a lot of "jargon" and we're going to tackle some more, so let's take a laugh break.

Medical Record Bloopers

"We have discussed her hemorrhoids. The bottom line is…"

"Patient has been married for 30 years, living at home with husband, and in the past has had dogs, cats, and children as pets."

"Duration of illness is probably at least since he became ill."

Ready to get back to it? Let's go.

Adherence to documentation standards creates an environment for quality patient care. Organizations and healthcare providers adopt and maintain rigorous documentation standards for other important reasons.

Think back to our examples at the beginning of the module. Do you remember the patient who had the wrong leg operated on? As you can imagine, this would not only ruin the patient's day, it would probably make for a long and frustrating day, week, month, and year for the healthcare provider. Quality, accurate healthcare documentation protects the patient, but it also protects the provider. The concept of applying medical, legal, and administrative operations within a healthcare organization to minimize the exposure to liability is known as **risk management**.

A good **risk management** program holds everyone—doctors, nurses, staff—accountable and reduces the risk of lawsuits and patient care errors.

Highlights

The concept of applying medical, legal, and administrative operations within a healthcare organization to minimize the exposure to liability is known as **risk management**.

Quality healthcare documentation practices minimize the potential for **fraud and abuse.** Individuals, state and local governments, as well as private insurance companies, spend billions of dollars annually for healthcare services. Excellent healthcare documentation means healthcare providers can support the medical bills with clear, accurate records and are more likely to receive full reimbursement for their services. Claims can be denied or payment reduced if complete, accurate documentation does not support the healthcare charges.

Government auditors and accrediting organizations look very closely at medical records to determine if the healthcare provider is changing, manipulating, or altering diagnosis or treatment records to receive inappropriate reimbursement. **Fraud and abuse** detection and prevention are benefits of a well-managed risk management program.

I. **FILL IN THE BLANK.**
   Using the word/word parts in the box, fill in the blanks.

   1. _____ is the concept of applying medical, legal, and administrative operations within a healthcare organization to minimize the exposure to liability.

   2. A good risk management program holds _____ accountable and reduces the risk of lawsuits and patient care errors.

   3. To minimize the potential for_____ quality healthcare documentation is a must.

   4. Fraud and abuse_____ are benefits of a well-managed risk management program.

detection and prevention
everyone
risk management
fraud and abuse

Physician Query

Sometimes as you transcribe and edit, you may find that the doctor has dictated an error. Maybe he mentioned a broken left arm in one sentence, and then talked about casting the right arm later. What's a transcription editor to do?

It will vary by your account instructions, but if those instructions require verbatim transcription editing, you'll go ahead and transcribe or edit it as it is. You will probably flag it as a mistake as well. But won't misinformation cause a problem for the patient and their record? It could, but luckily, there's someone to fix it.

Medical coders get the report you transcribe or edit. When they find an error, they have a tool called the **physician query** form. A physician query is used when the medical coding specialist requires additional information or a clarification to appropriately code the patient's medical record. In a small office, medical coders often have the ability to simply ask the physician. In larger offices or outpatient coding in a hospital or clinic setting, a form is used to request additional information from the physician.

The physician query becomes a permanent part of the medical record. When a physician responds to a physician query, the medical coder can use the information in the query as documentation for coding purposes.

So don't worry! These potential mistakes you're transcribing and editing will be fixed (even if you're not the one doing the fixing). We'll talk more about this later, but in the meantime let's look at some common errors.

Common Errors – Scenarios 1 and 2

Review the following report and answer the question below.

Medical Record

Procedure Note

PATIENT NAME:

MEDICAL RECORD NUMBER: 18-65-76

OPERATION DATE: 8/25/2001

SURGEON: Dr. Smith

PREOPERATIVE DIAGNOSIS: Obstruction in esophagus due to carcinoma.

PROCEDURE PERFORMED: Dilatation of esophagus and replacement of nasogastric feeding tube.

FINDINGS: This patient had radiation therapy for squamous cell carcinoma located in the mid thorax beginning at below the aortic arch. The radiation therapy has not opened the esophagus and the patient cannot swallow satisfactorily around the 18-French nasogastric tube. The patient was brought in for dilation of his esophagus and possible pharyngogastric tube insertion; however, the patient developed tachycardia and shortness of breath and it appeared that his condition was fragile.

It is known this patient has severe coronary artery disease with ejection fraction of 15% and cardiomyopathy of severe degree. Therefore, the procedure was stopped after dilating the esophagus up to 30-French.

The nasogastric tube, which was previously placed and pulled back up, was passed down into the stomach and fixed in this position. The patient tolerated the procedure satisfactorily, although the full extent of the planned surgery was not performed. The patient's pulse returned back to 100 with no change in blood pressure with nasal oxygen saturation remaining normal. The patient was sent to post-anesthesia care unit.

I. MULTIPLE CHOICE.
Choose the best answer.

1. What information is incorrect or missing from this report?

○ operation date
○ patient name
○ medical record number
○ preoperative diagnosis

Review the following report and answer the question below.

Medical Record

Clinic Note

PATIENT NAME: John Smith

MEDICAL RECORD NUMBER: 25-85-96

DATE: 2/18/2004

PHYSICIAN: Dr. Jones

HISTORY: This is a 54-year-old male with a history of seizure disorder, likely etiology was alcohol related. No history of head injury or coma. She has not had any seizures in more than six months. He has slowed down on his alcohol use and is complaining of some dizziness, usually worsened with a quick change in position. She has also quit smoking and is using the patch. He was on Neurontin, but it has been discontinued. He is currently taking doxepin 150 mg h.s.

Neurological exam is unremarkable, and there is no change from the previous visit.

ASSESSMENT: Dizziness

PLAN: If EEG (electroencephalogram) is negative, plan to give Antivert 12.5 to 25 mg p.o. p.r.n. for dizziness. Again, I stressed to her to stop drinking. His follow up appointment will be in six months.

I. MULTIPLE CHOICE.
Choose the best answer.

1. What information is incorrect or missing from this report?

○ patient name
○ date
○ gender inconsistency
○ medical record number

Common Errors – Scenarios 3 and 4

Review the following report and answer the question below.

Clinic Note

PATIENT NAME: Jane Jones

MEDICAL RECORD NUMBER: 25-87-52

DATE: 7/27/2000

PHYSICIAN: Dr. Smith

This 65-year-old lady was seen today 7/25/2000 in the ___ [PLACE] for evaluation of her MP joint. Her left great toe was submitted to a procedure on August 16th of last year for an advanced hallux rigidus deformity.

At the time of the operation, the spurs of the metatarsal head were properly removed, and the base of the proximal phalanx resected. An intramedullary pin and Kirschner wire were placed to maintain the joint space. Unfortunately, in the followup, the joint space completely obliterated and presently the appearance of the MP joint was back to its preoperative condition with the spur formation and only a slight shortening of the great toe. The bunion was properly removed, and the alignment of the great toe is very satisfactory.

On clinical examination, there is considerable tenderness over the MP joint of the great toe, and there is a very limited range of motion that is exceeding 5 to 8 degrees.

I explained to the patient that at this point in time only a fusion of the MP joint could relieve her of the pain and recommended such an intervention.

With her consent, I made arrangements for her to see Dr. ___ [NAME] in the first part of December for arrangement for this intervention.

In the meantime, I prescribed clog shoes to see how much relief of the symptoms they could afford.

I. **MULTIPLE CHOICE.**
   Choose the best answer.

   1. What information is incorrect or missing from this report?
      - ○ gender inconsistency
      - ○ patient name
      - ○ medical record number
      - ○ date inconsistency

Review the following report and answer the question below.

Operative Report

PATIENT NAME: Bob Smith

MEDICAL RECORD NUMBER: 29-85-11

OPERATION DATE: 4/25/2003

SURGEON: Dr. Johnson

PREOPERATIVE DIAGNOSIS: Right temple lesion.

POSTOPERATIVE DIAGNOSIS: Right temple lesion.

PROCEDURE: Excision of left temple lesion.

ANESTHESIA: Local.

SPECIMENS: Right temple lesion.

ESTIMATED BLOOD LOSS: 5 mL.

COMPLICATIONS: None.

INDICATIONS: Mr. ___ [NAME] presents with a right temple lesion which is ulcerating consistent with basal cell carcinoma.

OPERATIVE DESCRIPTION: After informed consent was obtained from the patient, he was taken to the operating room in the ___ [PLACE] and placed in the supine position and prepped and draped in the usual fashion. An elliptical incision was made following skin tension lines. The lesion was excised and sent to pathology for permanent section. Hemostasis was obtained with bipolar cautery.

The wound was closed in layered fashion with 4-0 Vicryl and 5-0 nylon running suture and dressed with Bacitracin.

II. MULTIPLE CHOICE.
Choose the best answer.

1. What information is incorrect or missing from this report?

   ○ surgeon name
   ○ patient name
   ○ operation date
   ○ none of the above

Unit 4
Patient Confidentiality

Patient Confidentiality – Introduction

Now that we've talked about documentation standards, risk management, and the role of the medical transcription editor in identifying and addressing common documentation errors, we're going to talk about another critically important issue and professional responsibility of the medical transcription editor: assuring patient confidentiality.

Think back to the Introduction of the last unit. We presented four scenarios to illustrate the importance of accuracy, timeliness, and confidentiality. The last scenarios illustrate the unforeseen, but potentially devastating, consequences of compromised record security and patient confidentiality.

Scenario 3:

Kelly visits a local clinic for blood work and learns she has AIDS. The clinic's computer is "hacked" into and her personal information and AIDS status are printed on an anti-homosexual flyer in her hometown.

Scenario 4:

Your husband suffers from depression. He is treated with medication and counseling and copes well with family and work. He applies for a promotion but it is denied because his boss heard from his neighbor, a nurse who works where your husband receives his medical care, about his depression and thinks it might affect his ability to do a good job.

In this unit, we are going to discuss patient confidentiality issues and the responsibility of the medical transcription editor with regard to protecting patient confidentiality. We'll first cover paper versus electronic health records and the impact of technology on confidentiality. We'll then take an in-depth look at HIPAA (Health Insurance Portability and Accountability Act), which is the comprehensive federal law that deals with patient confidentiality. Finally, we'll tie the unit together with a discussion of professional ethics in the medical records industry.

Are you ready? Let's talk technology and the medical record.

Technology and the Medical Record

Not so very long ago, when information in patient medical records was all stored on paper and was only transferable to other healthcare providers via confidential mail and private telephone calls, it was relatively difficult for outsiders to gain access to it. Of course, this meant it wasn't particularly easy for those who needed access to information to get it either! Healthcare providers, like consulting physicians and nurses, had to wait for the piece of paperwork to be found and shuffled around to get the information they needed.

Now information can be instantly transferred via e-mail, fax, Internet sites, voice files, video, and even small hand-held portable devices.

These miracles of modern technology have enhanced the opportunities for collaboration because patient information can be shared quickly for the best possible medical care available. It is really exciting to think about! You can be on vacation virtually anywhere in the world, and your provider can instantly access your records or otherwise exchange vital medical information on you with your hometown doctor. Especially for those with complex medical histories or multiple medical problems, this can mean the difference between life and death.

However, there's a tradeoff to having easily available information, and that tradeoff is **security**. The free flow of information means an increased risk of personal data and medical details being intercepted. Not a comfortable feeling, but there's no turning back—and we wouldn't want to. As long as the potential risks of electronically transferred data are managed, technology provides enhanced health information management and information sharing. First things first, though; let's get a good feel for the electronic health record then move on to an expanded discussion of confidentiality and security.

The **EHR**, or **electronic health record**, is a medical record that exists entirely in electronic format. A patient's EHR can be a compilation of information from a single visit or contain information from multiple healthcare-related visits. Most healthcare providers are somewhere in between an entirely paper-based system and a completely computer-based (electronic) system.

In the near future more and more healthcare providers will migrate to electronic health records to store and transmit their patients' health information. Standard accepted practices, known as **health informatics standards**, for collecting, maintaining, and transferring healthcare information among computer systems make it possible for healthcare providers to select and maintain an appropriate EHR system for their documentation needs.

> **Highlights**
>
> Technology has enabled exciting breakthroughs for patients and the medical community, such as video conferencing. Video conferencing allows physicians an opportunity to consult "face-to-face" with their patients, other professionals, or both. In some cases, video conferencing has enabled "supervised" medical procedures to be performed in remote areas under the direction of capable clinicians, nurses, or physicians. This technology has also been instrumental in saving lives.

> It's critical to note that there is currently no national standard electronic health record system. There is public and industry-wide discussion, and a generally widely held belief, that a "universal" electronic health record will be adopted in the future.

EHR Benefits – Lesson 1

There are many benefits for healthcare providers to switch from a **paper-based record** (medical record data printed and stored on paper in a hard copy format) to an **electronic-based record** (medical record data stored in an electronic format in a computer system or systems). These benefits include the following:

Ease of storage: The more visits a patient makes to his or her healthcare provider, the larger the patient's medical record becomes. Many healthcare providers see hundreds or even thousands of patients. Record storage can take up a lot of space in any office. Storing patient's health information in an electronic health record (EHR) simply saves space.

Accessibility: Authorized users can access EHR information from on-site or remote computers. If a healthcare provider needs information, they no longer have to physically go to a record storage area or request a file clerk retrieve documents from a physical record in a records room. Authorized users have immediate access to information. Information is stored and indexed for easy retrieval on demand.

Efficiency: Easy access leads directly to efficiency. As soon as information is entered, it's accessible. The end user (patient, physician) does not have to wait for the document to travel from healthcare provider to medical transcription editor to medical coder to medical biller before they have access to it. The original document is available and additions can be made efficiently until the document reaches a final form.

Searchability: It takes less time to search for a specific item in an electronic document than in a hard copy document. Software tools and features make searching quick and easy. This is a benefit for providing patient care to an individual patient and it is a time saver as well.

Systematized Nomenclature of Medicine (SNOMED) is a standardized medical vocabulary used to facilitate the indexing, storage, and retrieval of patient information in an electronic health record. The current version includes more than 150,000 terms. Just like a can of soda can be called soda pop, soft drink, Coke, or carbonated beverage—but they are all still a can of soda—medical language has different ways of describing the same thing.

Here's a simple example. A heart attack in medical language is a myocardial infarction. This can be recorded in a medical record as MI (myocardial infarction), cardiac infarction, myocardial infarct, heart attack, or in many other various ways. However, running reports to see how many people had "heart attacks" at your facility last year is a little complex when the diagnosis can be listed any number of ways!

SNOMED identifies myocardial infarction as the standard language for recording a heart attack diagnosis. Healthcare providers using electronic medical records software incorporating SNOMED would record each "heart attack" as a myocardial infarction. SNOMED makes indexing by diagnosis, treatment, or other important medical classification simpler and more user friendly (and more accurate).

Facilities, researchers, educators, and governments collect, sort, classify, and retrieve information. Compiling of statistics for cancer survival rates or cross-referencing of diagnosis/treatment information can be accomplished more readily with electronic health records. Many electronic health record (EHR) systems have adopted the SNOMED medical vocabulary.

As you can imagine, better information makes for better decisions, not only for individual healthcare providers' risk management plans, education, and other programs, but it is important for national healthcare issues. It helps agencies decide how to fund healthcare, how to spend research and development dollars, and how to respond to individual and national healthcare issues.

In 2003, new cases of cancer occurred at the following rates:

All sites combined: 477.2 per 100,000 people per year

Prostate: 171.5 per 100,000 men per year

Female breast: 127.6 per 100,000 women per year

Colorectal: 50.7 per 100,000 people per year

Lung: 64.8 per 100,000 people per year

If you are interested in learning more about SNOMED visit the following link:

I. **TERMINOLOGY.**
   Enter each term in the space provided. Read the definition and description for each term.

1. **ease of storage** _____

An EHR benefit that helps save space when storing records.

2. **accessibility** _____

An EHR benefit that offers easy and immediate access to information.

3. **efficiency** _____

An EHR benefit wherein information is accessible the moment it's entered to whoever needs it.

4. **searchability** _____

An EHR benefit that expedites the time it takes to search for an item and makes it easier to find.

5. **Systematized Nomenclature of Medicine** _____

(SNOMED) A standardized medical vocabulary used to facilitate the indexing, storage, and retrieval of patient information in an electronic health record.

6. **paper-based record** _____

Medical record data printed and stored on paper in hard copy format.

7. **electronic-based record** _____

Medical record data stored in an electronic format in a computer system or systems.

EHR Benefits – Lesson 2

Collaboration

Accessibility and efficiency make collaboration and information sharing easier. Many providers can simultaneously view a record simply by accessing the record electronically. This collaborative process—or the use of information technology to improve the quality, safety, efficiency, and confidentiality of healthcare through simultaneous access to patient health information by multiple healthcare providers—is known as **health information exchange**. You should remember this last definition, you will be tested on it later. Simply stated, it means patient care is better when everyone providing care has access to patient health information simultaneously.

Uniformity and Standardization

As mentioned previously, adoption of a national electronic health record system will take place in a matter of time. In the meantime, most electronic health record systems adhere to **structure and content standards**—common elements and definitions to be included in an electronic health record.

Imagine for a moment that you gave 20 different individuals a blank piece of paper and asked them to prepare a document describing a broken leg. No two papers would end up looking the same! One might begin with details of the accident. Another might begin with a description of the wound. It is very difficult to control or change the ordering of information, required information, or uniformity or standardization of information in the "paper" world.

On the other hand, electronic health record programs can control the order of information within a document and the order of documents within a file, can create required information fields, and can provide or restrict access to information so that users enter and update information in compliance with **health informatics standards**. The program sets the structure and content standards; the user must enter information in accordance with the structure and content standards.

Here is an example of an electronic health record template in which information is entered following a set structure and guideline:

Note there are fields grayed out so the information cannot be changed (like Site Code).

Note the items appear in a specified order and the order cannot be changed.

These same principles can be applied to the text of the document as well so that regardless of the dictated order, the information is entered and stored in a consistent order for each patient.

Reduction in Medical Errors

When records are available quickly, are easily searched, and updates are easy to make, the opportunities for patient care errors are reduced. Additionally, handwritten entries in a patient record can be challenging to read. (Have you ever tried to decipher a signature on your prescription slip?) A totally integrated EHR does away with handwritten entries and reduces the risk of errors made trying to decipher illegible scrawl.

I. TERMINOLOGY.
Enter each term in the space provided. Read the definition and description for each term.

1. **collaboration** _____

An EHR benefit wherein information sharing is made easier.

2. **health information exchange** _____

The use of information technology to improve the quality, safety, efficiency, and confidentiality of healthcare through simultaneous access to patient health information by multiple healthcare providers.

3. **uniformity and standardization** _____

An EHR benefit in which health record systems adhere to structure and content standards.

4. **structure and content standards** _____

Common elements and definitions to be included in an electronic health record.

5. **health informatics standards** _____

Structure and content standards that must be maintained in a health record.

6. **reduction in medical errors** _____

An EHR benefit wherein the opportunities for patient care errors are reduced.

EHR Challenges

We don't want to talk only about the roses and skip the thorns—so let's look at some of the challenges to be managed with electronic records.

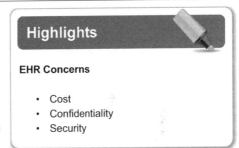

Highlights

EHR Concerns

- Cost
- Confidentiality
- Security

Cost

The main disadvantage to fully implementing an EHR is the cost. There is no national standardized EHR program (although this is an initiative being created at national, state, and local levels, as well as in industry groups, such as The Joint Commission). So designing, implementing, and maintaining an EHR is a significant undertaking. Healthcare providers must invest dollars to develop or purchase, then install and maintain an EHR system that adequately meets their needs.

Confidentiality and Security

The biggest concerns are maintaining confidentiality and security of the patient's health information. Identity theft and unauthorized use of personal information are constantly in the news. In fact, in 2006, there was a well-publicized case of a worker in a Veterans' Administration hospital who took home the personal data and medical information on thousands of veterans.

The Department of Veterans Affairs recently announced that a computer containing personal information on more than 26.5 million veterans and their spouses was stolen.

Initial reports stated that the information was on veterans discharged since 1975. Further reports revealed that the information on 30,000 active-duty Navy personnel and 20,000 National Guard and Reserve personnel were also "potentially included." Records at risk also included any veteran who left the service before 1975 but had submitted any VA claims.

Unfortunately, social security numbers were included in the information that was stolen, exposing veterans and their spouses to the potential of identity theft. The laptop containing the records was stolen from the Maryland home of a Department of Veterans Affairs analyst who was not authorized to remove the data from the VA office.

(AARP. www.aarp.com)

Let's face it. It would have been much more difficult for this data analyst to take home 26.5 million hard copy records!

A series of privacy laws over the years has sought to address the issues of security and confidentiality—eventually leading to the drafting and implementation of the **Health Insurance Portability and Accountability Act (HIPAA)**, the law that protects confidentiality and security of electronically transmitted information. There is a lot to be said about HIPAA, and we've just finished saying a lot about other things. It's probably a good time to have some exercises and review before you are ready to start absorbing more information.

I. MATCHING.
Match the correct term to the definition.

1. ____ health informatics standards

2. ____ electronic health record

3. ____ health information exchange

4. ____ Health Insurance Portability and Accountability Act (HIPAA)

5. ____ paper-based record

A. Record of a patient's health information which is created and stored in a computer.

B. Privacy law which protects the confidentiality of electronically stored health information.

C. Simultaneous access to a patient's health information to improve the quality of healthcare.

D. Medical record data printed and stored on paper.

E. Standards developed to collect and transfer healthcare information between computer systems.

II. TRUE/FALSE.
Mark the following true or false.

1. All healthcare providers use an electronic health record system.

   ○ true
   ○ false

2. An electronic-based record is recorded on an electronic device such as a tape recorder or digital voice system.

   ○ true
   ○ false

3. The use of information technology to improve quality, safety, efficiency, and confidentiality of healthcare through simultaneous access to patient health information by multiple healthcare providers is known as health information exchange.

   ○ true
   ○ false

4. The United States has a universal electronic health record system. Every provider who uses electronic health records must use the national system.

   ○ true
   ○ false

5. Electronic health record is a medical record which exists entirely in electronic form.

   ○ true
   ○ false

III. MULTIPLE CHOICE.
Choose the best answer.

1. Which of the following would not be considered a benefit when utilizing the electronic health record?

   ○ easy to store information
   ○ easy to locate information
   ○ easy access for family and friends
   ○ easy for other health professionals to read the medical record

2. The EHR makes it easier to_____.

   ○ read the physician's orders
   ○ get information about the patient from other healthcare facilities
   ○ get the patient's medical record quickly
   ○ all of the above

3. The standardized medical vocabulary used in indexing, storage, and retrieval of patient information in the EHR is known as:
   ○ SNOMED
   ○ uniformity and standardization
   ○ efficiency and accessibility
   ○ efficiency and searchability

4. When using systematized nomenclature to document a medical event such as a heart attack, which would be preferred?
   ○ cardiac heart attack
   ○ myocardial infarction
   ○ heart attack with severe chest pain
   ○ myocardial wall heart attack

5. Which would not be considered a problem associated with implementation of the EHR?
   ○ cost of designing, implementing and maintaining the electronic record
   ○ maintaining confidentiality
   ○ finding a place to store the electronic records
   ○ controlling access to the electronic record

Health Insurance Portability and Accountability Act (HIPAA)

Now that you have some background information, we can move on to HIPAA, patient privacy, and confidentiality.

The federal government has enacted a series of laws designed to protect an individual's privacy. These include The Privacy Act of 1974, The Privacy Act of 1993, and the **Health Insurance Portability and Accountability Act** of 1996, which is generally known as **HIPAA**.

The Privacy Acts of 1974 and 1993 are general laws designed to protect an individual's right to keep private matters private. These include information related to one's employment, religion, or medical history. You are probably aware that doctors are "not allowed" to give any detail of your medical problems or history to anyone not involved in your care or not authorized by you. For many years, the healthcare industry operated with a fairly clear understanding of the nature and extent of these laws, as well as any penalty which may result from a failure to comply with them.

According to HIPAA, privacy is a "fundamental right" which "speaks to our individual and collective freedom."
(Federal Register, Vol. 65. No. 250. Thursday, December 28, 2000. Rules and Regulations. p. 82465.)

But what does that really mean? The Fourth Amendment guarantees "the right of the people to be secure in their persons, houses, papers and effects…" In other words, the Constitution specifically protects all of us from information about our private lives being made available in the public domain.

In 1996, the federal government decided that the existing laws were insufficient to deal with the reality of the threat technology poses to privacy, and specifically to the privacy of a patient's health record. The government believes that not having a guarantee of privacy has a detrimental effect on receiving effective medical care. Basically, if you are afraid that your health information is going to be made public, you may not tell your physician what is really wrong, have tests that are important to your care and treatment, or even go to a practitioner at all.

There has been quite a bit of press coverage (especially in the healthcare documentation industries) about the resultant legislation—HIPAA. (This is pronounced as one word "hippa.") Although it was passed in 1996, the time frame for healthcare organizations, insurance companies, facilities, and practitioners to become compliant was April 14, 2003.

I. **MULTIPLE CHOICE.**
   Choose the best answer.

1. HIPAA was instituted in what year?
   - ○ 1974
   - ○ 1993
   - ○ 1996
   - ○ 2003

2. The Privacy Acts of 1974 and 1993 keep what private?
   - ○ employment information
   - ○ religious information
   - ○ medical history
   - ○ all of the above

3. Why was HIPAA brought about?
   - ○ there were no existing laws to deal with privacy
   - ○ existing laws were insufficient to deal with the threat technology posed to privacy
   - ○ the Privacy Acts already in place had nothing to do with medical records
   - ○ to allow doctors to give out details of private information about their patients

4. All healthcare organizations had to become HIPAA compliant by what year?
   - ○ 1974
   - ○ 1993
   - ○ 1996
   - ○ 2003

What is HIPAA?

Within the Privacy Rule portion of HIPAA, there are three reasons given as justification for HIPAA:

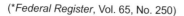

1. To protect and enhance the rights of consumers by providing them access to their health information and controlling the inappropriate use of that information.
2. To improve the quality of healthcare in the U.S. by restoring trust in the healthcare system among consumers, healthcare professionals, and the multitude of organizations and individuals committed to the delivery of care.
3. To improve the efficiency and effectiveness of healthcare delivery by creating a national framework for health privacy protection that builds on efforts by states, health systems, and individual organizations and individuals.*

(*Federal Register, Vol. 65, No. 250)

In other words, the goals of HIPAA are:

Goals of HIPAA

1. Give people access to their own health information and control others' access.

2. Enable patients to trust the healthcare system to keep their medical records confidential.

3. Make healthcare better and more efficient by putting privacy protection into a national framework.

There are four major reasons provided in the Privacy Rule as to why the government believes that these changes are necessary. These include:

Reasons for HIPAA

1. More organizations are involved in the provision of care and the processing of claims.

2. The growing use of electronic information technology.

3. Increased efforts to market healthcare (and other products) to consumers.

4. Increased availability of highly sensitive medical information due to advances in scientific research.

In many ways, technology has dramatically improved healthcare. Specifically, the means of retrieving and sharing information allows physicians to take better care of their patients. As we discussed earlier, however, there are inadvertent and often unintentional side effects of the availability of information. For example, as technology improves and businesses, healthcare facilities, and individuals upgrade their equipment, old computers often still contain private information. It is possible that a doctor could sell (or even give away) an old computer without realizing that confidential records are still accessible. There is also more sinister and deliberate mismanagement of patient information. Some specific examples of clear breaches to privacy which contributed to the need for HIPAA are cited in the Privacy Rule. Here are a few of them:

- The *Ann Arbor News* reported in February 1999 that a Michigan-based health system accidentally posted the medical records of thousands of patients on the Internet.
- The *New York Times* reported in August 1991 that a speculator bid $4,000 for the patient records of a family practice in South Carolina. Among the businessman's uses of the purchased records was to sell them back to the former patients.
- The *National Law Journal*, May 30, 1994, cited a banker who also sat on a county health board gained access to patients' records and identified several people with cancer and called in their mortgages.

Frightening, isn't it? HIPAA, at least ideally, should curtail some of these privacy breaches. It provides penalties—both civil and criminal—for the misuse of private medical information. Civil penalties can be incurred of not more than $100 per violation, totaling not more than $25,000 per year. Criminal penalties are much stiffer. A basic violation can include a fine of up to $50,000 and/or up to a year in prison. Using health information under false pretenses can carry penalties of up to $100,000 and/or five years in prison. Violations involving the use of private health information for commercial gain or malicious harm can carry fines of up to $250,000 and/or 10 years in prison. In other words, the rule has some teeth.

If you are interested in learning more about the HIPAA Privacy Rule, you can read all or part of the ruling. It can be accessed by visiting the following link.

http://www.hhs.gov/ocr/privacy/hipaa/administrative/

When you visit the webpage, notice that under Privacy Rule, you can choose if you want to view the rule in PDF, Text, or HTML. They are further separated into parts. Determine how you want to view the document and begin by clicking on **part 1** of the appropriate format.

As a medical transcription editor you will be handling, reading, and interpreting people's private medical information every day. You will need to have a fundamental understanding of HIPAA rules and its applicability to your job. This will be important in three primary ways:

1. Privacy notices
2. Internal facility policies
3. Confidentiality

Let's examine each of these in more detail.

HIPAA Privacy Notices

Medical practitioners and facilities are now required by the new law to inform patients of their rights under it. Most places that you visit for healthcare will give you a document generally called a "Notice of Privacy Practices." This outlines what the specific policies regarding compliance to the law are at that facility.

The following is an example of a privacy notice:

> We've placed a multi-page visual aid in the appendix on pages 163-170.

In addition to physically providing you with their notice, the facility should require that you acknowledge you received it. This means that you have to sign a paper which basically says, "I acknowledge that I received (the facility's) Notice of Privacy Practices."

The following is an example of an acknowledgment:

We've placed a visual aid in the appendix on page 171.

As a medical transcription editor, you should know about this acknowledgement as it relates to a patient's health record.

Internal Facility Policies

The Privacy Rule requires that all facilities, businesses, and individuals who have access to health records abide by the rule (obviously). As a medical transcription editor, you fall under this category. Wherever you ultimately work as a transcription editor, the place you work will have created a series of policies and procedures that will put them into compliance with HIPAA regulations.

First and foremost among these is the necessity of you being trained on your employer's specific policies. This is actually part of the Privacy Rule—the requirement that all new employees are appropriately trained for compliance with the rule.

Beyond that, although everyone is required to comply with the Privacy Rule, each employer, facility, or organization will ultimately determine how he or she satisfies the law. You will then be expected to abide by the policies and procedures of your employer.

Because you are working with medical information all the time, there are many aspects of your job that will be potentially controlled by policies related to HIPAA. Some of these include:

- Access control
- Transfer of data
- Use of the Internet
- Offsite work
- Storage of health information
- Audits

As you can see, there are many possible ways that HIPAA may affect your job as a medical transcription editor. The good news is that as an employee you will not have to define and implement the policies for compliance. You need to learn and practice them, but your employer will have to be totally familiar with the law and make sure that everyone understands and does their best to abide by their policies and procedures.

Access control – This would include protecting patient information from people who should not have access to it. This may be actual paperwork that needs to be in a locked room (to which you have a key) or may be electronic information on a computer that you will be required to keep secure. HIPAA may actually determine where in the office the medical records are located, limiting access to foot traffic within the facility.

Transfer of data – It may be necessary for you to get additional information from physicians as part of your job. The method and manner of the transfer of this data will be determined by specific policies, ensuring that it is always done securely.

Use of the Internet – There will be predetermined policies and procedures for connection to the Internet (for any reason) from a computer containing confidential patient information. This will allow protection of that information from viruses or hackers attempting to gain access to any computer connected to the Internet.

Offsite work – It may be that you have the ability to work as a medical transcription editor from home. This would create specific HIPAA concerns which would need to be addressed by your employer.

Storage of health information – A patient's record needs to be stored for future use in the care of that patient. After you have finished using the record for transcription editing purposes, you will follow specific guidelines for its storage.

Audits – It may be the case that you or your facility is selected for an audit by an outside organization. While some auditors require (and are allowed) access to all aspects of a patient's records, it may also be necessary for you to "scrub" records of confidential patient information. You should know the policies and procedures for de-identifying records.

I. **MATCHING.**
Match the correct term to the definition.

1. ____ Protecting patient information from people who should not have access to it

2. ____ Method and manner of getting additional information from physicians and to insurance companies

3. ____ Policies and procedures for connecting to the Internet from a computer containing confidential patient information

4. ____ Concerns that would arise if you will be working from home

5. ____ Guidelines for storage of patient records for future use

6. ____ Policies and procedures for de-identifying records

A. use of the internet
B. audits
C. transfer of data
D. access control
E. storage of health information
F. offsite work

HIPAA and Patient Confidentiality

The third and most substantial way that HIPAA will impact your job as a medical transcription editor is through patient confidentiality. You already know HIPAA was enacted by the federal government to protect patient privacy. If you have received any healthcare services in the last few years, you should be somewhat familiar with HIPAA notices and policies. These are an effort by healthcare providers to comply with HIPAA standards.

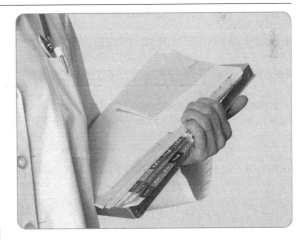

In fact, if patients are afraid their health problems will impact either their jobs or their position in the community, they will be much less likely to give accurate answers to questions asked by their practitioner regarding any health problem, and they may entirely avoid seeking professional help for it.

It makes sense. Patients should be able to trust their doctors to keep confidences. Most people are aware a physician, nurse, or other type of practitioner is required to keep their patient information *strictly* confidential. After all, this notion has been reiterated over and over again in the movies and on television. But how does that extend to you as a medical transcription editor working in a health information management (medical records) department, reading patient records?

First and foremost, you will have to be familiar with and abide by the policies and procedures of your facility. You should also be required to sign a confidentiality form stating that you understand records are confidential and that you will abide by the policies and procedures of the facility/employer. Employers generally go about this in one of two ways:

1. You sign and date an actual copy of the policy statement with all details spelled out on the part of the form you affix your signature to.
2. You receive a separate copy of the policies and procedures of your employer and sign an acknowledgement that you did receive it and you read it.

The following is a sample of a policy statement with a place for employee signature (As described in #1):

> We've placed a multi-page visual aid in the appendix on pages 172-173.

The following is a sample of the type of form you may be required to sign acknowledging you received the policy statement of your employer:

> We've placed a visual aid in the appendix on page 174.

Of course, looking at an acknowledgment statement is fairly useless without a copy of the policies you are acknowledging. Although these will vary, they will contain much of the same information that appeared in the first sample. The information will be presented differently because it will not be in the first person.

The following is a sample confidentiality statement:

> We've placed a visual aid in the appendix on page 175.

Your Part in Patient Confidentiality

Although the policy statements for every place you work will differ, the individual components should be largely the same. It will be important for you to understand what the individual issues are, the terminology associated with confidentiality, and the applicability to your position.

Let's assume you work with patient records every day—confidential patient records. You see their names, numbers, addresses, medical histories, current problems, and family histories. In other words, all manner of private information.

Some of the records you read will be interesting. Very interesting. Interesting to the point that you will want to talk to others about them. This is a really good dish! You've got to hear this! *Avoid the temptation*. If you do speak to anyone outside of the healthcare professionals who are also managing the patient's care about information contained in a medical record, you must *never* discuss it using the names or *any other identifying details* of the patient.

You have to be careful because it is possible to make clear who a patient is without ever saying the patient's name or age. For example, you could say, "A middle-aged white male from Texas whose father was also president of the United States…" No names. No dates. No age. Who is being discussed?

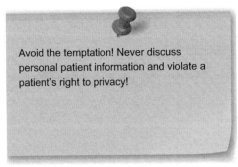

Avoid the temptation! Never discuss personal patient information and violate a patient's right to privacy!

It's a small world—the friend you speak with might be the brother of a cousin's friend of a former spouse's sister—you can't know. It's important to be absolutely exact in maintaining patient confidentiality. After some exercises, we'll come back and wind up this module with a few more important things to know about patient confidentiality, including when information can be released and confidentiality in patient interaction.

Review: HIPAA

I. **MULTIPLE CHOICE.**
Choose the best answer.

1. Privacy is _____.
   - ○ a fundamental right
   - ○ covered in the 4th amendment
   - ○ to be protected
   - ○ all of the above

2. When did the implementation of HIPAA become mandatory?
   - ○ in 1974
   - ○ in 1993
   - ○ in 2003
   - ○ in 1996

3. Within the Privacy Rules, which is not a justification for HIPAA?
   - ○ Protect consumer rights by providing access to their medical records.
   - ○ Control the inappropriate use of that information.
   - ○ Restore trust in the government.
   - ○ Create a national framework for health privacy protection.

4. Which is not considered a reason for implementation of HIPAA rules?
   - ○ Advances in scientific research and increased use of electronic technology.
   - ○ Increased desire to market healthcare products to the consumer.
   - ○ More insurance companies handling medical claims.
   - ○ Restrict healthcare provider's ability to file medical claims.

5. Preventing breach of privacy is one of the primary goals of the Privacy Rule. Which would be considered a breach of privacy?
   ○ Sharing medical information between physicians.
   ○ Providing information to third-party payers.
   ○ Leaving your work computer on when you take a break.
   ○ Faxing medical information to a physician caring for a patient previously seen in your facility.

6. Working as a medical transcription editor requires knowledge about policies and procedures of your employer. These would include _____.
   ○ access control
   ○ transfer of data
   ○ use of the Internet
   ○ all of the above

7. Which would not be considered a violation of confidentiality?
   ○ Providing your sign-on code and password to a friend.
   ○ Using another person's sign-on code and password.
   ○ Accessing information about your neighbor who is a patient in the hospital.
   ○ Accessing the patient's medical record to code an operative report.

8. Violating Privacy Rules can result in _____.
   ○ loss of your job
   ○ a major fine
   ○ going to jail
   ○ all of the above

9. A Statement of Policy usually includes which of the following?
   ○ A formal job description for a medical transcription editor.
   ○ Your financial remuneration as a medical transcription editor.
   ○ Penalties for breach of the policy.
   ○ The responsibility of employees.

10. An acknowledgment of responsibility is _____.
    ○ a statement of the employee's legal and ethical guidelines
    ○ a form provided to the patient to be signed
    ○ a list of what treatment the patient will receive
    ○ a list of the rules to be followed at the facility

Consent to Release Medical Information

After the serious nature of the previous discussion, it seems to be time for another laugh.

Medical Humor

A patient in New York went to a doctor for a checkup. The doctor wrote out a prescription for him in his usual illegible handwriting. The man put it in his pocket and forgot to have it filled. Every morning for two years he showed it to the conductor as a railroad pass. Twice it got him into the Radio City Music Hall, once into a baseball park, and once into a symphony concert. One day he mislaid it at home, and his daughter picked it up, played it on the piano, and won a scholarship to a music conservatory.

Now, back to business. There are two primary ways in which consent can be given by the patient for medical and personal information to be released—written and implied.

Written consent is when a patient signs a **release of information (ROI)** form authorizing his/her healthcare provider to release or send medical information to a particular individual or another healthcare provider for a specific purpose. These forms are most commonly used: 1) when patients need to have their information sent to a new healthcare provider (most often encountered when changing providers); 2) when patients are referred to a specialist for additional or consulting care that cannot be provided by their general practitioner; 3) when a lawsuit is in process and access to vital medical information is needed by attorneys; 4) to allow the healthcare provider to submit medical claims to insurance companies for reimbursement and to answer any questions they may have regarding the patient's medical care, diagnoses, or prognosis. There are many other reasons written consent will be needed in order to transfer a patient's confidential medical information—all of which cannot be listed here.

Implied consent is when a patient consents to disclosure of confidential medical information without signing an official release of information form. This type of consent usually occurs when patients are seen and treated in medical settings that require those who assist with their care to be informed of their conditions and treatment plans (e.g. assisting physicians, surgeons, nurses, and technicians). Consent is also implied when patients are transferred from one healthcare provider or medical facility to another and the new provider or medical facility must have access to the patient's medical information in order to ensure continuation of care.

There are times a provider may legally disclose confidential patient information without either written or implied consent and not get into trouble. These situations are both legally and ethically justifiable due to overriding social considerations or concerns. These are normally safety issues, such as patients who are threatening serious bodily harm or injury to others or to themselves. In these instances, the attending physician or healthcare professional is justified in notifying the proper authorities and/or even the intended victim(s) of such a possibility. Additionally, patients who have contracted communicable diseases are also to be reported immediately to the Center for Disease Control so proper disease controls can be implemented to keep the disease from spreading and infecting many individuals. There are some instances in which social concerns outweigh patient privacy and confidentiality issues.

As a medical transcription editor, you will be hearing and seeing information about patients that is considered private and personal. Such information, if not kept confidential, can cause problems not only for the patient, but for the provider as well.

I. MULTIPLE CHOICE.
Choose the best answer.

1. A patient must sign this form to authorize the healthcare provider to release medical information.
   - ○ written consent form
   - ○ release of information form
   - ○ implied consent form
   - ○ no form needs to be signed

2. Which of the following is NOT a common reason to give written consent of a release of medical records?
   - ○ when attorneys need access to vital information for a lawsuit
   - ○ when you want your sister, a nurse, to review your records
   - ○ when your doctor refers you to a specialist for additional care
   - ○ when you change healthcare providers and information needs to be sent to them

3. When a patient consents to disclosure of confidential medical information without signing anything it is called _____.
   - ○ written consent
   - ○ release of information
   - ○ implied consent
   - ○ doctor consent

4. Which of the following is a situation where confidential information can be released without written or implied consent?
   - ○ when the patient transfers to another healthcare provider
   - ○ when attorneys need access to vital information for a lawsuit
   - ○ when your doctor refers you to a specialist for additional care
   - ○ if you contract a communicable disease and the Center for Disease Control needs to be notified

Unit 5
Medical Record Work Types

Medical Record Work Types – Introduction

The medical record, whether inpatient or outpatient, is the *who, what, where, when,* and *how* of patient care. In general, a patient's medical record is made up of some or all of the following types of reports.

Report Type	Classification	Sample Headings
Clinic Note	Medical Clinic Multispecialty Clinic	Subjective Objective Assessment Plan
Progress Note	Medical Clinic Multispecialty Clinic Acute Care/ Hospital	Subjective/History of Present Illness Objective/Physical Examination Assessment Plan
Letter	Medical Clinic Multispecialty Clinic Acute Care/ Hospital	Does not typically use headings except the typical greeting and salutation.
Emergency Room	Acute Care/ Hospital	Chief Complaint History of Present Illness Past Medical History Allergies Current Medications Review of Systems Physical Examination Laboratory Findings Assessment and Plan Discharge Instructions
History and Physical	Acute Care/ Hospital	Chief Complaint History Of Present Illness Past Medical History Allergies Current Medications Social History Family History Review of Systems Physical Examination Laboratory Data Admitting Diagnosis or Assessment Plan

Consultation	Multispecialty Clinic Acute Care/ Hospital	Referring Physician Reason for Consultation Chief Complaint History of Present Illness Past Medical History Physical Examination Laboratory Data Assessment Recommendations
Operative Note	Acute Care/ Hospital	Preoperative Diagnosis Postoperative Diagnosis Operation Performed Surgeon Anesthesia Estimated Blood Loss Complications Indications for Operation Findings Description of Operation
Procedure Note	Medical Clinic Multispecialty Clinic Acute Care/ Hospital	Preoperative Diagnosis Postoperative Diagnosis Procedure Performed Surgeon Indications for Procedure Findings Description of Procedure
Discharge Summary	Acute Care/ Hospital	Admitting Diagnosis History of Present Illness Past Medical History Social History Family History Review of Systems Physical Examination Laboratory Data Hospital Course Discharge Diagnoses Discharge Medications Disposition
Radiology	Medical Clinic Multispecialty Clinic Acute Care/ Hospital	Clinical History Report Type Impression
Pathology	Multispecialty Clinic Acute Care/ Hospital	Clinical History Gross Examination Microscopic Examination Diagnoses

I. TRUE/FALSE.
Mark the following true or false.

1. A clinic note generally contains the headings of Chief Complaint and Hospital Course.
    ○ true
    ○ false

2. If the doctor does not dictate all headings, the transcription editor is free to insert the ones he or she sees fit.
    ○ true
    ○ false

3. The four main headings one might see in a clinic note are Subjective, Objective, Assessment, and Plan.
    ○ true
    ○ false

4. A letter done in the transcription editing setting typically uses headings and/or subheadings.
    ○ true
    ○ false

5. Report components are always the same in medical reports.
    ○ true
    ○ false

6. The term *medical record* is applied to both inpatient and outpatient types of reports.
    ○ true
    ○ false

7. The heading of Family History is only found on the history and physical report.
    ○ true
    ○ false

8. One of the headings a transcription editor can expect to encounter on a radiology report is Gross Examination.
    ○ true
    ○ false

9. In simple terms, the *who, what, when, where,* and *how* of a patient comprises the medical record.

⭘ true

⭘ false

10. Both operative notes and procedure notes usually have a preoperative diagnosis as well as a postoperative diagnosis dictated.

⭘ true

⭘ false

Clinic Notes and Acute Care Work Types

Typically, the work type is tied to the kind of facility rendering care. If, for example, you perform transcription editing for an outpatient facility (medical clinic, radiology clinic, multispecialty clinic), you would generally edit clinic notes, letters, radiology reports, progress notes, and some procedure notes. If, however, you edit for an inpatient facility (hospital), you would most likely spend your days (or nights) editing history and physicals, progress notes, consultations, operative notes, procedure notes, discharge summaries, ER Reports, and some radiology reports. Of note, pathology reports are often edited by MTEs who specialize in pathology. To that end, they are not included in this breakdown. In a very general and

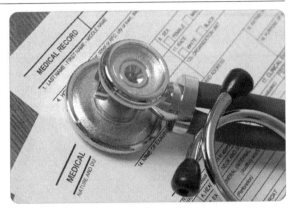

broad way, we often classify transcription editing into two levels—Clinic Notes and Acute Care. In fact, the practicum modules in this training program are broken down into clinic notes, basic acute care, and advanced acute care modules. Let's break it down by the work types you will likely be exposed to most.

Clinic Note

Medical clinics and a variety of multispecialty clinics use the SOAP (pronounced soap) formatting for reports. This is a quite common method of formatting routine or problem-oriented physician visits.

SOAP stands for **S**ubjective, **O**bjective, **A**ssessment, and **P**lan.

History and Physical (H&P)

If you work on an acute care account you will likely edit your fair share of these reports. H&Ps are generated upon patient admittance to the hospital and are used for reference throughout the hospital stay. An H&P's primary function is to provide background information on new patients and outline what is planned for the hospital stay.

Consultation

A consultation is done when a physician other than the attending physician (or the attending service) examines and/or performs tests on a patient. It is not uncommon for a patient admitted to the hospital to undergo several consultations from more than one specialist.

Operative Note

An operative report (or procedure note) is generated upon completion of any type of surgical procedure. These are required for same-day surgeries and admitted patients.

Discharge Summary

Just as a patient admitted to the hospital has an admission history and physical, they are also required to have a discharge summary. A discharge summary contains all the information found in the history and physical, plus the hospital course and discharge plans. This, as the name implies, is a summary of all that happened before the patient was discharged.

Emergency Room (ER) Reports

Emergency departments provide urgent care to patients. Patients treated in emergency departments and discharged the same day are considered hospital outpatients. The increased use of emergency room services for more routine care has resulted in a large volume of healthcare documentation for ER outpatients.

Radiology Report

A radiology report is any type of an x-ray examination. These include, but are certainly not limited to, chest x-rays, backs, hips, arms, feet, toes, fingers, skull, CT and MRI examinations, upper GIs, ultrasounds, bone age tests, etc. They typically follow a relatively simple format.

Now let's take a closer look at some sample reports from the various work types. This exposure will help you put the information you have learned in this unit so far into context.

Clinic Note

To review, medical clinics and a variety of multispecialty clinics use clinic notes in the SOAP format for medical reports. This is a quite common method of formatting routine or problem-oriented physician visits. When you go to your family physician, a clinic note is generated. When you visit your dermatologist for your annual skin care screen (You do this, right? Especially those of you in our sunshine states?), a clinic note is generated. It is likely that you will edit a lot of clinic notes in your career as an MTE, and it is definite that you will edit them in this training program!

Medical Record

SUBJECTIVE: Status post removal of multiple large lesions. The patient returns for recheck of excision site and pathology results.

OBJECTIVE: Everything is healing well. She is having a little bit of separation or scabbing in the area of the most significant tension portion of the flap on her thigh; however, it should still heal well. Everything is intact. Everything is healing well. She has good circulation.

ASSESSMENT: Status post removal of multiple large lesions, healing well.

PLAN: We will exchange her Steri-Strips in all areas. She will need to continue to change these Steri-Strips or Hypafix tape. She was given a good supply of both hypoallergenic Steri-Strips and Hypafix along with Mastisol. The larger bottle of Mastisol, not the small bottle, will be given to her and will be charged separately as alternative medical supplies.

Other than that, she is healing well, and the pathology was discussed with her. Specifically, I spent considerable time discussing the dysplastic nevus, which was removed. However, the surgical margins were clear, so no further excision will be done at this point.

Medical Record

SUBJECTIVE: This 50-year-old white male, established patient at this facility, hurt his shoulder about a month ago and also has an intermittent right sciatica. He has been using two 800 mg Motrin tablets 3 times a day without relief. He quit his alcohol use just before Christmas.

OBJECTIVE: Vital signs show blood pressure 137/83, weight 152, temperature 98.3, and pulse 69. There is tenderness of the left posterior shoulder, made worse by elevation. There is also faint tenderness of the neck. There is no palpable lumbosacral tenderness. Straight leg raises are negative. Strength is adequate in all extremities.

ASSESSMENT

1. Left shoulder pain.
2. Sciatica.

PLAN

1. Discontinue ibuprofen.
2. Naprosyn 500 mg 1 tablet twice a day with food as needed for back pain. Patient was counseled to take one of these twice a day, and if he does not see some improvement within 2 weeks to return to see me. He was also counseled not to use this longer than 2 weeks.
3. The patient was offered to take blood work today to check his kidneys and liver, although he refused this due to another commitment. He has to get back to work.
4. Return if symptoms persist. Otherwise, schedule followup appointment in 2 weeks.

History and Physical

When a patient is to be admitted to the hospital, a history and physical examination is performed. The document typically includes the patient's past medical history, and often the family and social history, and outlines any medications the patient is taking. The physician completes a detailed review of systems, performs a comprehensive physical exam, and usually orders tests, x-rays, and lab work related to the patient's condition or symptoms [for example, an electrocardiogram (EKG), chest x-ray, comprehensive blood panel, etc.]. An assessment of medical problems is typically included, as is a plan for management and treatment. If the projected hospitalization includes plans for a surgical procedure, this report may also be called a "Preoperative History and Physical."

CHIEF COMPLAINT: Left inguinal hernia.

HISTORY OF PRESENT ILLNESS: This established patient is a 59-year-old male who has a 3-month history of a tender left inguinal hernia. The patient first noticed this problem last fall. The patient describes the pain as being constant but mild. The hernia is reducible. The patient reports the hernia is also warm; however, the patient denies any changes in bowel or bladder habits, any blood in the urine or stool, or any nausea or vomiting. Patient also denies any change in stool caliber.

PAST MEDICAL HISTORY: The patient has hypercholesterolemia, as well as tinnitus. Tinnitus was diagnosed last year.

PAST SURGICAL HISTORY: The patient has had a sinus operation 15 years ago.

ALLERGIES: THE PATIENT HAS NO KNOWN MEDICAL ALLERGIES.

CURRENT MEDICATIONS: The patient takes gemfibrozil 600 mg p.o. b.i.d., ibuprofen 800 mg p.o. t.i.d. p.r.n., and simvastatin 20 mg q.h.s.

SOCIAL HISTORY: The patient has never been a smoker. The patient denies alcohol use and other illicit drug use as well. The patient has been divorced for 3 years and currently lives by himself. He has 3 children, all sons.

FAMILY HISTORY: Negative for coronary artery disease, strokes, cancer, and diabetes.

REVIEW OF SYSTEMS: The patient reports he has had approximately a 10% weight loss in the past couple of months; however, this weight loss has been permissible. Otherwise, review of systems is noncontributory. The patient denies chest pain, palpitations, or syncope. Denies shortness of breath or wheezing. Denies nausea or vomiting. Denies headaches or syncope.

PHYSICAL EXAMINATION: General: This is a 59-year-old white male, awake, alert, and oriented x3, very pleasant to talk to, who is sitting comfortably in a chair in no acute distress. Vital signs: Temperature 97.0, heart rate 75, respiratory rate 20, blood pressure 156/101. Patient has a 98% saturation on room air. HEENT: Head is normocephalic, atraumatic. Pupils are equally round and reactive to light and accommodation. Extraocular muscles are intact. There is no icterus. Mucous membranes are moist. Neck: Supple with good range of motion. Trachea is midline. There was no JVD or lymphadenopathy present. Chest: The lungs are clear to auscultation bilaterally. Heart: Regular rate and rhythm without murmur. Abdomen: Soft, nontender, and nondistended. Bowel sounds are present. Extremities: Warm. There is no clubbing, cyanosis, or edema noted. GU exam: Patient has a readily apparent left inguinal hernia. The sac will pulse or bulge with any increase in intra-abdominal pressure. The hernia is reducible. It is also tender to palpation. Rectal exam: The patient has normal sphincter tone. There is stool present in the vault; however, there is no gross blood present on examination. Prostate is enlarged but soft.

ASSESSMENT: The patient is a 59-year-old white male who is here for a preoperative history and physical. The patient is otherwise healthy.

PLAN: The patient is scheduled to have a left inguinal hernia repair done tomorrow.

HISTORY OF PRESENT ILLNESS: This is a 78-year-old white male, established patient, with a past medical history significant for coronary artery disease with 3-vessel CABG and atrial flutter who was admitted for medical cardioversion using propafenone.

The patient developed an atrial flutter after undergoing a CABG procedure 8–9 years ago. Previously the patient was DC cardioverted for the atrial flutter. The patient did respond to the DC cardioversion and returned to a normal sinus rhythm for 3 weeks. However, the patient eventually reverted back to an atrial flutter rhythm after being cardioverted. The patient then underwent an ablation therapy for the atrial flutter but the procedure was unsuccessful.

The patient is currently asymptomatic at this time. However, the patient's symptoms are usually confined to lethargy during episodes of regular heartbeat that he can notice. The patient denies any paroxysmal nocturnal dyspnea, any orthopnea, or any decrease in exercise tolerance.

PAST MEDICAL HISTORY

1. Three-vessel coronary artery bypass graft.
2. Bilateral carotid endarterectomies.
3. Left femoral-popliteal bypass.
4. Atrial flutter refractory to sotalol, DC cardioversion, and ablation therapy.
5. Diabetes mellitus.
6. Hyperlipidemia.
7. Hypertension.

FAMILY HISTORY

1. Mother died of Hodgkin's disease.
2. Father died at age 94 due to natural causes.
3. No siblings who had any history of heart disease.
4. No family history of hypertension or diabetes mellitus type 2.

SOCIAL HISTORY: The patient has a 120-pack-year history for smoking. The patient is a social drinker and he denies any illicit drug use.

MEDICATIONS: Admission medications include Coumadin 3 mg per day, simvastatin 30 mg at night, potassium chloride 10 mEq every other day, ranitidine 150 mg at night, nitroglycerin sublingual p.r.n. for chest pain, metoprolol 50 mg b.i.d., felodipine 5 mg daily, glipizide 2.5 mg every morning, digoxin 0.125 mg daily, and nitroglycerin patch 0.2 mg remove at night.

The patient had an echocardiogram showing an ejection fraction of 65% and concentric LVH.

REVIEW OF SYSTEMS: General: The patient denies any fevers, chills, and excessive weight gain or weight loss. The patient denies any recent history of trauma or headaches. Eyes: The patient denies any discharge from the eyes, itchiness of the eyes, or double vision. Ears: The patient denies any discharge from the ears or tinnitus. Nose: The patient denies any rhinorrhea or difficulty breathing. Throat: The patient denies any thyromegaly or difficulty swallowing. Cardiovascular: The patient denies any paroxysmal nocturnal dyspnea, orthopnea, or decrease in exercise tolerance. Respiratory: The patient denies any history of TB, pneumonia, or shortness of breath. Gastrointestinal: The patient denies any blood in stools, any diarrhea, constipation, nausea, or vomiting. Endocrine: The patient denies any excessive weight gain or weight loss, any excessive heat or cold intolerance. Neurological: The patient denies any seizures, numbness, tingling, or memory loss. Renal: The patient denies any polyuria, dysuria, or difficulty urinating.

PHYSICAL EXAMINATION: Vital signs showed a pulse of 54, blood pressure 123/68, temperature 97.5, and a respiratory rate of 14. In general, the patient is alert and oriented with no acute distress, and is a well-developed, well-nourished male. HEENT revealed a patient who has a normocephalic, atraumatic head. Extraocular muscles are intact. Pupils were equal, round, and reactive to light bilaterally. No evidence of jugular venous pulsations. No thyromegaly, no scleral icterus, and no evidence of lymphadenopathy. Cardiovascular examination revealed S1 and S2 to be present with a regularly irregularly heartbeat and distant heart sounds. No murmurs, gallops, or rubs were appreciated. Lungs showed clear to auscultation bilaterally with good air entry bilaterally. No accessory muscles were being used. No rales, rhonchi, or wheezing was appreciated. Abdominal examination showed no tenderness, no distention, no masses, and positive bowel sounds. Extremities revealed no clubbing, cyanosis, or edema. Pedal pulses were present and there was evidence of scars secondary to the fem-popliteal procedure. Neurological examination showed cranial nerves 2–12 to be grossly intact, and no focal deficits.

ASSESSMENT/PLAN: Atrial flutter. The patient will be converted using propafenone. Cardiology will start this medication and titrate appropriately. We will restart the patient on his home medications. We will obtain serial EKGs in the morning. The patient will also get blood results of PT, INR, PTT, basic metabolic panel, magnesium, and phosphate, and Cardiology will continue to follow this patient.

Consultation

To review, a consultation is done when a physician other than the attending physician (or the attending service) examines and/or performs tests on a patient. It is not uncommon for a patient admitted to the hospital to undergo several consultations from more than one specialist. Consultations often include a REFERRING PHYSICIAN and a REASON FOR CONSULTATION heading.

Medical Record

REASON FOR CONSULTATION: Right lower lobe lung nodule.

HISTORY OF PRESENT ILLNESS: Patient is an established 63-year-old white male with a 2-year history of squamous cell T4 N0 M0 pharyngeal tumor treated with chemotherapy and radiation therapy, which was complicated by post radiation dysphagia resulting in permanent J-tube placement.

Last week he had a chest x-ray, which revealed a new right lower lobe 3 cm lung nodule, which was confirmed by CT scan that revealed a peripheral lung nodule. Patient stated his weight has been stable and he feels well.

A CT-guided needle biopsy is scheduled by ENT. We were asked to evaluate to see if another option is to do a bronchoscopy for this nodule.

ALLERGIES: None.

MEDICATIONS: He takes occasional Tylenol.

SOCIAL HISTORY: Quit tobacco 1–1/2 years ago. He smoked 2 packs per day for 40 years. Moderate alcohol use. No drug use. He was a painter for 40 years without airway protection.

FAMILY HISTORY: He has a grandmother with breast cancer.

REVIEW OF SYSTEMS: No fevers, chills, or night sweats. Has gained weight. No headaches. HEENT: No visual or auditory changes. Positive sinus problems. Positive dysphagia since radiation. Had a barium swallow which revealed that his pharynx would never close appropriately for eating; therefore, he is fed through a permanent J-tube. Neck: Positive pain secondary to radiation. Chest: No chest pain, palpitations, edema, or orthopnea. Lungs: Had PFTs last week. He does have some dyspnea on exertion and occasional cough. GI: No hematochezia, melena, nausea, or vomiting. No abdominal pain. He has a J-tube in place. GU: Negative. Musculoskeletal: Negative. Skin: Negative.

PHYSICAL EXAMINATION: General: Vitals per electronic note. He is a thin white male who appears to be in no acute distress. Neck has hard skin changes secondary to radiation. No lymphadenopathy. Very limited range of motion. HEENT: Tympanic membranes were normal. Nasal mucosa had some clear rhinorrhea and pale mucosa. Unable to fully open mouth, therefore unable to evaluate the posterior pharynx, but did have a normal-appearing mucosa from what could be seen. Heart: Regular rate and rhythm. No murmurs, rubs, or gallops. Lungs are clear to auscultation bilaterally. No wheezes, rhonchi, or rales. No retractions noted.

LABORATORY DATA: Pulmonary function tests showed a normal FEV1 of 4.21, which is 121% of predicted. FEV1/FVC of 80. Lung volumes and diffusion were normal.

ASSESSMENT/PLAN: Right lower lobe peripheral lung nodule. Suspect metastatic squamous cell carcinoma. We will get a needle biopsy, which is already scheduled for next week by his ENT. We will present his case to determine further course of action after diagnosis obtained from CT-guided needle biopsy.

Medical Record

HISTORY OF PRESENT ILLNESS: The patient is an 11-year-old white female who suffered a bad biking accident today, with multiple abrasions, and embedded foreign body into the multiple abrasions on her face, torso, and hands.

The only injury, which is gaping open, is a very extensive avulsion laceration of her lower lip, with severe trauma to her lower incisor dental area with some fractures involving the base of the teeth. They did make an appointment for today, to see their dentist for their tooth-related problem; however, she does have a very complex laceration extending entirely through her orbicularis oris muscle, with some avulsion of the buccal gingival area, which will require some flap closure of the gingiva. This will also be pertinent for survival of the teeth, by maintaining adequate blood supply to the area. She presents today upon referral from her primary care physician for consultation and potential repair.

PAST MEDICAL HISTORY: The patient states that she is otherwise healthy with no other medical problems.

PAST SURGICAL HISTORY: Denies any significant past surgical history.

ALLERGIES: No known allergies.

MEDICATIONS: None.

SOCIAL HISTORY: Nonsmoker, nondrinker.

FAMILY HISTORY: Negative for hemophilia. Both parents are alive and well and so are all her siblings with no chronic illnesses or conditions.

REVIEW OF SYSTEMS: As noted above, otherwise negative.

PHYSICAL EXAM
GENERAL: Well-developed, well-nourished afebrile patient.
NEUROLOGIC: Normal affect and mood. Alert and oriented x3.
EYES: Pupils are equally round and reactive to light. Extraocular movements are intact.
HEAD/EARS/NOSE/MOUTH/OROPHARYNX: Traumatic-appearing face. Ears, nose, and oropharynx are without abnormality. The head, face, lips, and mouth are as noted in HPI with lacerations and abrasions.
NECK: Supple, full range of motion. No adenopathy. No thyroid gross abnormality.
LUNGS: Clear to auscultation and percussion. Normal respiratory effect.
HEART: Regular rate and rhythm, without murmur.
CARDIOVASCULAR: No gross edema, or significant varicosities.
ABDOMEN: Soft, nontender, nondistended. No hepatosplenomegaly or masses. Normal bowel sounds.
EXTREMITIES: Within normal limits.
MUSCULOSKELETAL: Generally unremarkable. Normal gait. No asymmetry. Normal range of motion.
LYMPHATIC: No adenopathy, neck and axilla.
SKIN: No visual or palpable gross irregularities on areas examined. She has no tendon injuries.

ASSESSMENT/PLAN: Biking accident today, with multiple abrasions, embedded foreign body into the multiple abrasions on her face, torso, and hands, and a gaping extensive avulsion laceration of her lower lip, with severe trauma to her lower incisor dental area, and with some fractures involving the base of the teeth.

PROCEDURE: Debridement, as well as possible, was done of all the abrasions and embedded foreign bodies throughout the areas. Topical anesthetic was placed so that the patient could shower at home and further clean the areas. She will continue to put antibiotic ointment on these areas as well. Surgical intervention will be acutely required for the avulsion of the buccal gingiva on her lower lip and repair of the large laceration extending through the orbicularis oris muscle of the lip.

PLAN: We will take the patient to the operating room immediately for repairs to be done on an outpatient basis. The risks, complications, and alternatives of the procedures have been explained to the patient and her mother and all their questions answered. The patient's mother signed the consent to proceed with surgery.

Operative Note

Each time an operation or procedure is performed, an operative report or procedure note is generated. This document lists important information, such as the preoperative and postoperative diagnoses, type of operation, reason for operation, description of operation, and findings.

Medical Record

PREOPERATIVE DIAGNOSIS: Left ureteral stricture.

POSTOPERATIVE DIAGNOSIS: Left ureteral stricture.

OPERATION PERFORMED: Left ureteral stent change under anesthesia.

DRAINS: 7 French hydrophilic microvasive 24-cm left ureteral stent.

INDICATIONS: The patient is a 49-year-old white male who has left ureteral stricture secondary to colon cancer and radiation. He has frequent calcification of his stents and needs them changed every 2 months. He presents for change.

DESCRIPTION OF PROCEDURE: Consent was obtained. The patient was given an IV sedative, placed on the operating table in the dorsal lithotomy position, and prepped and draped in the usual sterile fashion. The urethra was anesthetized with 2% Anestacon. The 21 French cystoscopic sheath and 4 oblique lens were placed into the bladder under direct vision without difficulty. The left ureteral stent was identified and removed using alligator forceps. The 21 French cystoscopic sheath and 4 oblique lens were then placed into the bladder under direct vision again. Using the glide wire the left ureteral orifice was cannulated. Plain films showed good position of the tip of the glide wire in the left renal pelvis. The stent was then passed over the guide wire and pushed in place using a pusher and the guide wire removed. There was one full turn left in the bladder. Plain film confirmed good position of the stent. The bladder was emptied, and the scope was removed. The patient was taken out of the lithotomy position, moved under his own power to a gurney, and transported to the recovery room in stable condition. There were no complications, and the patient tolerated this procedure well.

Medical Record

PREOPERATIVE DIAGNOSIS: Nevus of the midback and nevus of the left lower back.

POSTOPERATIVE DIAGNOSIS: Nevus of the midback and nevus of the left lower back.

PREOPERATIVE SIZE: Midback 0.8 x 0.6 cm; left lower back 0.6 x 0.4 cm.

POSTOPERATIVE DEFECT SIZE: Midback 3.0 cm; left lower back 0.6 cm.

PROCEDURE: Excision of nevus, mid-lower back with complex layer closure; punch biopsy of nevus, left lower back.

DESCRIPTION OF PROCEDURE: The relevant risks and aspects, as well as the rights of refusal were explained to the patient. The informed consent was obtained and placed on the chart.

The patient was brought to the operating suite, and the two areas on the back were prepped and draped in the usual sterile manner. A fusiform shape was drawn around the lesion on the mid-lower back. The area was then infiltrated with anesthetic. A #15 scalpel was used to excise down to the level of subcutaneous fat. The tissue was removed and sent to pathology. The edges were undermined with blunt scissor dissection. Hemostasis was maintained with electrocautery. The subcutaneous layer was closed with 3 sutures of 4-0 Vicryl. The cutaneous layer was reapproximated with a running suture of 4-0 nylon. A 6-mm punch biopsy was used to remove the nevus of the left lower back. The subcutaneous layer was reapproximated with one suture of 4-0 Vicryl. The cutaneous layer was closed with 3 sutures of 4-0 nylon.

ANESTHESIA: 5 cc of lidocaine with 1:100,000 epinephrine.

ESTIMATED BLOOD LOSS: Minimal.

COMPLICATIONS: None.

DISPOSITION: The patient was alert and oriented times 3 post procedure and tolerated the procedure well. He was given both verbal and written wound care instructions. He is to follow up on Friday at 8:30 a.m. for suture removal.

Discharge Summary

A discharge summary is the report generated when a patient is being discharged from an inpatient hospital admission. The patient's name is listed, as well as the admission date and discharge date, although this information has been stripped from most of the files you will deal with in this training program in an effort to protect patient confidentiality. A brief history explaining why the patient was admitted is presented here, as well as a generalized description, although a detailed description of the patient's hospital course (what was done and why during the hospital stay) is preferred. A final diagnosis is included and a listing of any and all procedures performed during the patient's hospital stay.

Medical Record

CHIEF COMPLAINT: Monocular diplopia and blurry vision, OD, secondary to cataract.

HISTORY OF PRESENT ILLNESS: Monocular diplopia and blurry vision, OD, secondary to cataract.

PAST MEDICAL HISTORY: Positive for rheumatoid arthritis, hypothyroidism, and chronic open angle glaucoma.

PAST SURGICAL HISTORY: Status post benign breast mass excision, total abdominal hysterectomy.

SOCIAL HISTORY: She denies use of tobacco and alcohol.

MEDICATIONS: Timoptic b.i.d. OU, levothyroxine 0.075 mg daily, quinine 325 mg p.r.n. cramps, amitriptyline 25 mg at bedtime, Plaquenil 200 mg b.i.d., estrogen 0.625 mg daily.

ALLERGIES: She has a questionable allergy to oral antibiotics; however, she does not know which antibiotic.

REVIEW OF SYSTEMS: Noncontributory.

PHYSICAL EXAMINATION: Other than ocular, physical exam is within normal limits. Ocular exam: 20/40+, OU. She glares to 20/50 in both eyes. Tonometry by applanation at 0900, 14 and 16 mmHg respectively. The pupils are equal. Anterior segment exam is normal in both eyes. Dilated fundus exam: Lens reveals she has 2+ nuclear sclerosis with cortical changes in both eyes, somewhat more severe in the right than the left. Cup-to-disc: 0.4 with temporal sloping, OU. Disc is normal, OU. Macula normal, OU; periphery normal, OU.

DISCHARGE DIAGNOSES

1. Cataract, right eye.
2. Rheumatoid arthritis.
3. Hypothyroidism.
4. Chronic open angle glaucoma.

PROCEDURE: Phacoemulsification with posterior chamber IOL, right eye.

DISCHARGE MEDICATIONS

1. Tylenol with codeine 1-2 q.4-6 hours p.r.n. pain.
2. Diamox Sequels 500 mg p.o. q.1600 and at bedtime.

Medical Record

DIAGNOSES

1. Fracture of the inferior ramus of the pubis on the right.
2. Heme positive stool.
3. Anemia.
4. Dementia.
5. Weight loss.

HISTORY OF PRESENT ILLNESS: The patient is a 71-year-old male who had fallen somehow the night before admission. He had landed sitting, facing his bed, and he complained of his right leg hurting and not being able to walk. He usually could walk and exercise and was quite vigorous. He was seen last year for organic brain syndrome, but had no physical disability. He was on Motrin for occasional arthritic pain. He has a long history of weight loss and was to be admitted for barium enema electively the day after his presentation to the emergency room. He denied pain but was unable to stand.

PAST MEDICAL HISTORY: His weight has gone from 97 pounds to 92 pounds in 3 months. He had a urinary tract infection which showed no growth but was symptomatic. He has anemia with a hemoglobin of 11 noted 3 months ago. He has a history of organic brain syndrome with paranoia. He is status post left cerebral artery aneurysm, for which he had surgery. Following this he has had his organic brain syndrome. He is status post TURP for urinary retention and elevated PSA.

MEDICATIONS: Motrin p.r.n.

ALLERGIES: No known allergies.

SOCIAL HISTORY: He lives with his wife, and his children live next door.

REVIEW OF SYSTEMS: He had no complaints other than inability to stand.

PHYSICAL EXAMINATION: Older man who was sitting up with his right hip flexed at 45 degrees, externally rotated, and his knee flexed 45 degrees. He was moaning with exploration, but that is his usual. Temperature 96.9, pulse 78, respirations 18, blood pressure 150/62. Exam was essentially negative. Rectal was heme positive with normal prostate. His right leg was as described above. He was able to straighten the leg but could not rotate it to neutral. He could not weightbear. He was tender over the anterior ramus of the pubis on the right. Otherwise his extremities were normal except for being wasted.

LABORATORY DATA: Hemoglobin 9.3, hematocrit 28, with 17.6 lymphs and a white count of 5.2. Chemistries were normal except for an albumin of 3.3. X-ray showed a crack in the inferior ramus on the right.

HOSPITAL COURSE: The patient was admitted and put on bedrest. X-rays were reviewed with the radiologist, who agreed that there was a fracture of the inferior ramus of the pubis. The patient was discussed with orthopedics, who felt that gradual increase in weightbearing with a walker was best for him. He was seen by dietary who felt that he was at 84% of ideal body weight. He was given Enrich supplement. He did not have a large amount of pain. He had his barium enema as had been previously scheduled. He showed no gross pathology, but it was a limited study. After the barium enema the patient was able to weightbear and appeared happy and with minimal pain. He was discharged to home.

PROCEDURES: Barium enema, walker education.

DISCHARGE INSTRUCTIONS: He was set up for a followup appointment. He was to take an iron rich diet. After his followup it will be decided whether or not he needs to have iron supplements.

DISCHARGE MEDICATIONS: Motrin 400 mg p.o. t.i.d. three months supply and a walker were dispensed.

CONDITION AT DISCHARGE: Improved.

Emergency Room

Because patients treated in the emergency room are treated for such a wide variety of problems, it would be impossible to give you an example of everything you could expect to encounter. However, the format for emergency room report is basically the same everywhere and for all types of problems, unless they are extremely severe, in which case the patient will be admitted.

CHIEF COMPLAINT: Thrown from horse with loss of consciousness.

HISTORY OF PRESENT ILLNESS: This is an apparently 16-year-old female who was riding a horse today and was thrown, striking her head. She apparently was knocked out for 1 to 2 minutes, and after that awoke, being somewhat combative and confused. She was brought by ambulance here to the emergency department.

PHYSICAL EXAMINATION: This 16-year-old girl is in no acute distress, although she is intermittently somewhat confused and minimally combative. She has blood and fluid coming out of her left ear. No distal neurologic deficit is noted on gross exam. Cranial nerves 2–12 are grossly intact as well. Deep tendon reflexes 2+ and equal bilaterally. No focal or lateralized deficits are demonstrable. Chest is clear. Breath sounds are bilaterally equal without rales, rhonchi, or wheezes. No rib tenderness is noted. Her abdomen is soft, nontender, without guarding, masses, or organomegaly. Bowel sounds are active.

LABORATORY: Noncontrast CAT scan reveals pneumocranium on the left, with some edema of the left temporal lobe.

DIAGNOSIS: Cerebral contusion with basilar skull fracture.

ER TREATMENT: The patient's status was discussed with the attending physician. We elected to admit her to the ICU unit and monitor her for 24 hours.

CHIEF COMPLAINT: Altercation with facial injury.

HISTORY OF PRESENT ILLNESS: This is a 46-year-old lady who complains that she was hit in the face with a fist. This occurred at 2:15 a.m. She was hit multiple times. She had no loss of consciousness. She says that the right side of her nose and upper lip are numb. She has mild soreness of the left shoulder and left thigh.

PAST MEDICAL HISTORY: Negative.

MEDICATIONS: None.

ALLERGIES: None known.

IMMUNIZATION STATUS: Not current.

PHYSICAL EXAMINATION: Vital signs: Temperature 98, pulse 88, respirations 20, blood pressure 120/76. This is a well-developed, well-nourished Caucasian female who is alert and oriented times 3. Head, eyes, ears, nose, and throat exam is significant for tenderness at the left mandibular angle. There is some ecchymosis present here as well and pain with attempted motion of the jaw. The right mandibular condyle is somewhat tender as well. There is some right infraorbital tenderness, swelling, and anesthesia. Pupils are equal, round, reactive to light. There is no entrapment of upper gaze. In fact, the extraocular movements are intact in all directions. There is minimal amount of nasal tenderness, which is not clinically significant. Head, eyes, ears, nose, and throat exam is otherwise negative with hemotympanum. There is mild tenderness and swelling of the right posterior parietal scalp. There is also some mild tenderness of the left deltoid laterally and the lateral hips. Range of motion is quite good with both joints, that is, left shoulder and left hip. Distal neurovascular exam is intact. There is no neck, chest, back, or pelvis tenderness. Heart has regular rate and rhythm without murmurs. Lungs are clear to auscultation bilaterally. Abdomen is soft and nontender.

DIAGNOSTIC STUDIES: X-ray studies of the mandible and face reveal fracture of the left side of the mandible through the base of the coronoid process and most probably through the neck as well, along the base of the neck. It appears nondisplaced. Facial x-rays reveal an air/fluid level in the right maxillary sinus. No distinct fracture line is identified. Serum pregnancy test is negative.

ER TREATMENT: A CT was done to determine the exact site of maxillary sinus fracture and the exact nature of the mandibular fracture. The patient is turned over at this time, 8:20 in the evening, to the attending service, who will obtain the results of the CT and coordinate the patient's further care.

Radiology

The radiology report documents the type of x-ray that was performed, what the radiologist saw when viewing the film(s), and the final impression of the x-ray by the radiologist. The radiologist rarely takes the x-rays. However, he/she always interprets them and generates a report that is sent back to the ordering physician. Many clinics and specialty practices have their own radiology technicians who perform standard x-rays in-office and then the physician (not a radiologist) reviews the films and interprets them. Many types of x-rays, such as CT scans, MRIs, upper GI series, OB ultrasounds, nuclear scans, and more, are performed in the hospital setting simply due to the cost of owning the equipment to perform such radiologic procedures. In these circumstances the films are reviewed by the radiologist and a report is generated back to the ordering physician.

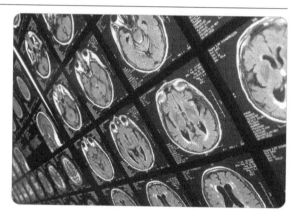

Medical Record

CLINICAL HISTORY: A 52-year-old patient status post thoracentesis, rule out pneumothorax.

PORTABLE CHEST X-RAY: There is no evidence of pneumothorax. There is no opacification of the right lower hemithorax compatible with effusion.

IMPRESSION: No evidence of pneumothorax.

CLINICAL HISTORY: Not dictated.

ABDOMINAL ULTRASOUND: Extremely limited exam was performed in correlation with the recently performed MRI. Patient did not present with a full bladder, and therefore the pelvis was not evaluated in detail. Again noted is the hydronephrosis of the right kidney with an ill-defined, hypoechoic density that extends caudal to the right kidney into the pelvis, best seen with the patient in the left lateral decubitus position. On reviewing the MRI, this mass correlates with the location of the right iliopsoas muscle.

IMPRESSION

1. Right flank mass, which extends caudal to the right kidney into the pelvis, which is poorly defined but can be identified by ultrasound, and therefore ultrasound can be used for localization for needle biopsy.
2. Repeat ultrasound with full bladder may be warranted.

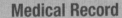

CLINICAL HISTORY: Large right frontal mass on CT scan in patient with left upper lobe lung lesion, question metastasis versus primary tumor.

MRI OF THE BRAIN

PROCEDURE: Sagittal T1 weighted images were obtained through the brain, followed by proton density and T2 weighted images in the axial plane. These were followed by axial T1 weighted images pre and post Magnevist injection.

FINDINGS: There are multiple enhancing lesions noted in both hemispheres of the brain. The largest lesion is in the right frontoparietal region near the gray/white junction. This lesion demonstrates extensive white matter edema with mass effect upon the frontal horn of the right lateral ventricle and mild right-to-left shift. Two smaller lesions are noted, one in the posterior left parietal region and a second in the anterior left temporal region. These lesions also enhance with gadolinium.

IMPRESSION: Multiple enhancing lesions in both cerebral hemispheres, consistent with metastatic disease. The largest of these lesions in the right frontoparietal region has extensive surrounding white matter edema with mass effect and mild right-to-left shift.

Unit 6
Report Components

Report Components – Introduction

Now that we have discussed the type of reports you will be exposed to, it makes sense to jump into report components. You can think of report components as "ingredients" needed to make a "cake"—or the medical record itself. If we break down the medical record we can inspect each component and put it back together again with a better understanding of how it goes together.

While all report types do not follow one specific template of headings, there are general headings associated with each work type. This will make more sense as we work through the examples in this unit. Let's begin with clinic notes.

Clinic Note Components

As you have learned, clinic notes are broken down into SOAP format, and are often even referred to as such. SOAP is an acronym for the first letter of each heading in the report:

S – SUBJECTIVE
O – OBJECTIVE
A – ASSESSMENT
P – PLAN

Some accounts use a format that includes the same information as the SOAP format, but the headings are different, and some use a combination of SOAP and other headings. Alternative headings include, but are not limited to:

HISTORY
PHYSICAL EXAMINATION
DIAGNOSIS
RECOMMENDATIONS

When editing clinic notes you will find that some dictators will not even say the entire heading but will recite only the letter instead. For example, the dictator might say "S colon" for the subjective heading. Depending on the account instructions, you might expand this out to SUBJECTIVE: or you might simply edit this as S:. It is also the case that many dictators use the basic SOAP format, but they never dictate any headings at all. In this case account instructions will often dictate whether you add headings or edit the report verbatim (with no headings). If you are to add the appropriate headings when required, it is essential to know what each heading is actually describing. Let's break them down.

Medical Record

SUBJECTIVE: A narrative of the patient's own description of his/her complaints. This would include any past history or review of systems, allergies, or medication lists that are provided.

OBJECTIVE: The description of the physician's findings on observation and examination, any physical signs, and laboratory testing or diagnostic studies, such as x-rays.

ASSESSMENT: How the physician interprets the findings (both subjective and objective). In other words, this is the physician's opinion, impression, assessment, or diagnosis.

PLAN: For treatment and followup. This includes any medication regimen, instruction (such as elevation or cleansing), suggested education, and followup instruction.

I. MULTIPLE CHOICE.
Choose the best answer.

1. The A in the SOAP formula stands for *Assessment*, which indicates _____.
   - ◯ Treatment and followup, including medication regimen, instruction, suggested education, and followup instruction.
   - ◯ How the physician interprets the findings; an opinion, impression, assessment, or diagnosis
   - ◯ A narrative of the patient's own description of his/her complaints: a past history, review of systems, allergies, or medication lists
   - ◯ The description of the physician's findings on observation and examination, any physical signs, and laboratory testing or diagnostic studies, such as x-rays.

2. The P in the SOAP formula stands for *Plan*, which indicates _____.
   - ◯ Treatment and followup, including medication regimen, instruction, suggested education, and followup instruction
   - ◯ How the physician interprets the findings; an opinion, impression, assessment, or diagnosis
   - ◯ A narrative of the patient's own description of his/her complaints: a past history, review of systems, allergies, or medication lists
   - ◯ The description of the physician's findings on observation and examination, any physical signs, and laboratory testing or diagnostic studies, such as x-rays

3. The S in the SOAP formula stands for *Subjective*, which indicates _____.
   - ◯ Treatment and followup, including medication regimen, instruction, suggested education, and followup instruction
   - ◯ How the physician interprets the findings; an opinion, impression, assessment, or diagnosis
   - ◯ A narrative of the patient's own description of his/her complaints: a past history, review of systems, allergies, or medication lists
   - ◯ The description of the physician's findings on observation and examination, any physical signs, and laboratory testing or diagnostic studies, such as x-rays

4. The O in the SOAP formula stands for *Objective*, which indicates _____.
   - ◯ Treatment and followup, including medication regimen, instruction, suggested education, and followup instruction
   - ◯ How the physician interprets the findings; an opinion, impression, assessment, or diagnosis
   - ◯ A narrative of the patient's own description of his/her complaints: a past history, review of systems, allergies, or medication lists
   - ◯ The description of the physician's findings on observation and examination, any physical signs, and laboratory testing or diagnostic studies, such as x-rays

Standard Acute Care Components

Acute care reports are the documentation for patient care rendered in an inpatient setting. The standard acute care reports (H&P, discharge summary, consults, and even ER reports) will include information such as the reason the patient is being cared for, the patient's history, the current condition, evaluation, diagnostic evaluation, treatment, assessment of condition, and plan going forward. This information will typically fall under one of the headings listed below, although there are other headings or report components used in acute care reports. Again, a thorough understanding of what information falls under each component will help you put together a more accurate document—which will effectively help you become a high-quality MTE. You can have your cake and eat it, too!

Medical Record

CHIEF COMPLAINT: The chief complaint, as the name implies, is the principal or main concern, issue, or reason for being seen. In a consultation report this might be referred to as REASON FOR CONSULTATION, but they mean the same thing. The information following this heading tells us why the patient is being seen, for example: a sprained ankle, heart palpitations, a motor vehicle collision, a peanut in the nose, etc.

HISTORY: The history information in a medical record is frequently broken down into a number of history categories (each generally with their own headings). The content under history headings gives us vital information regarding what treatment has been received in the past, medication history, pertinent family history, and even social history. You can surely imagine how historical information might be used to assess, treat, and diagnose a patient. For example, if a patient comes in with what could feasibly be either indigestion or chest pain, and this patient has a strong family history of congestive heart failure and myocardial infarction, a cardiac workup might be the first evaluation planned.

PAST MEDICAL HISTORY: This is where the past illnesses, diseases, and conditions are listed. This information can be presented in paragraph format or in a list.

SURGICAL HISTORY: This heading will hold information regarding a patient's past surgical history, frequently with dates included.

FAMILY HISTORY: The information under this heading includes information regarding family history of coronary artery disease, strokes, cancer, and diabetes. This will also frequently list whether family members and siblings are living or deceased.

SOCIAL HISTORY: This heading often holds information with regard to marital status, children or no children, employment status and occupational history, hobbies, military service, living arrangements, family structure/dynamics, smoking history, and alcohol use history (sometimes dictated as ETOH).

MEDICATIONS: This heading, as you might suspect, lists medications the patient is or was taking. Alternate medications headings include things like: CURRENT MEDICATIONS, MEDICATIONS LIST, or even MEDICATIONS ON ADMISSION. Sometimes this information is presented in a paragraph and other times in a list. There is much acceptable variation to how drug information is presented.

ALLERGIES: It is very important to document any allergic reactions a patient might have had to medications (or things like latex) to avoid administration of such medications in the future. In fact, many accounts will require any allergy statements BE PRESENTED IN ALL CAPS. A phrase common to the allergy heading is NO KNOWN DRUG ALLERGY. Frequently the allergen is listed with a description of the reaction it evokes.

REVIEW OF SYSTEMS: The review of systems, when fully utilized, is a fairly comprehensive overview of symptoms by body system. These are subjective findings (unlike the physical exam which relates objective findings). Systems commonly covered in the ROS include general/ constitutional, skin, eyes/ears/nose/mouth/throat, cardiovascular, respiratory, GI, GU, musculoskeletal, neurologic, and lymphatic. While these subheadings are not used all the time, they are the most common systems referenced in the ROS.

PHYSICAL EXAMINATION: The physical exam is the examination of the body for signs of disease or changes. The PE can be presented in stacked format with headings left-justified or in paragraph format with subheadings embedded throughout the paragraph. Account instructions will typically decide how the information is presented. While the headings may change in a given PE, the exam usually starts at the head and ends with the extremities. The physical exam headings typically include: vital signs, general appearance, HEENT, neck, lungs, heart, abdomen, genitalia, musculoskeletal, neurologic, skin, and extremities. We will take a much closer look at the physical examination in a later unit.

DIAGNOSTIC STUDIES: Information in the diagnostic studies headings typically includes laboratory data, x-ray, or other diagnostic testing. We will take a much closer look at laboratory data in a later unit, including types of lab values and normal ranges.

HOSPITAL COURSE: Evaluation and treatment rendered in the hospital is presented under this heading. In an ER report this might be referred to as ER TREATMENT.

DIAGNOSES/ASSESSMENT: As the name implies, the information under this heading includes the cause or nature of the condition or reason for being seen. These findings are frequently presented in a list format. It is generally preferred to not use abbreviations under the diagnoses heading. For example, if a dictator states "DIAGNOSIS: GERD," this would be expanded out to DIAGNOSIS: Gastroesophageal reflux disease.

PLAN: This heading holds information regarding future treatment and followup. In a discharge summary, the plan might be referred to as DISCHARGE INSTRUCTIONS.

I. FILL IN THE BLANK.
Using the word/word parts in the box, fill in the blanks.

1. This category is often broken down into several more detailed categories. _____

2. In the _____ section, the doctor notes that John is an unmarried college student who does not smoke or drink.

3. The section that indicates evaluation and treatment rendered in a hospital is under the heading _____.

4. _____ is the section that gives a comprehensive overview of symptoms by body system.

5. John comes in complaining of stomach pain. This is an example of the _____.

6. The _____ section is where the body is examined for signs of disease or changes.

7. John has a history of stomach ulcers. This would be indicated under _____.

8. The _____ section includes information that John is not currently taking any prescribed medicine.

9. The section that holds information regarding future treatment and followup is _____.

10. Information regarding John's past surgery would be indicated under _____.

11. The heading labeled _____ includes the cause or nature of the condition or reason for being seen.

12. In the _____ section, it is indicated that John's mother has a history of acid reflux problems.

13. The _____ section typically includes lab data, x-ray, or other testing.

14. This section indicates that John has NO KNOWN DRUG ALLERGY. _____

Allergies
Social History
Family History
Diagnosis/Assessment
History
Surgical History
Plan
Medications
Past Medical History
Diagnostic Studies
Physical Examination
Chief Complaint
Review of Systems
Hospital Course

Operative Note Components

Operative reports and procedure notes do not follow the same standard format as most other acute care reports. To review, an operative report (or procedure note) is generated upon completion of any type of surgical procedure. These are required for same-day surgeries as well as on admitted patients. The patient's name, medical record number, date of surgery, surgeon, and place of surgery are all listed on the report, but for our purposes (and to protect patient confidentiality) this information has been removed.

 **Medical Record**

PREOPERATIVE DIAGNOSIS: A preoperative diagnosis is listed to show the probable diagnosis, rule out a diagnosis, or state an unconfirmed diagnosis prior to the procedure.

POSTOPERATIVE DIAGNOSIS: The postoperative diagnosis lists the diagnosis made after the surgery is performed and the surgeon has had the opportunity to explore the diseased body area or organ system thoroughly to pinpoint the problem.

OPERATIONS: This is a very important part of the operative report—it lists all of the surgical procedures (in order of priority) that were performed on the patient during this particular operation.

SURGEON: The physician who performed the surgery.

ASSISTANT SURGEON(S): Any assistant surgeons who were present and assisted the primary surgeon with the operation(s).

ANESTHESIA: The type of anesthetic used, when applicable.

ESTIMATED BLOOD LOSS: The amount of blood loss during the operation/procedure, when applicable.

INDICATION FOR OPERATION: This gives background information on why an operation is being performed. This also frequently lists the consent statement—acknowledgement of the patient (or patient's caretaker) giving verbal or written consent to the operation and an understanding of possible complications.

PROCEDURE: This is an actual description of what occurred during the surgery. It is a minute-by-minute description of the proceedings of the surgery in the order they occurred, the techniques used, and the equipment and supplies used to carry it out.

FINDINGS: The findings section lists the outcome of the surgery, specifying what was found to be the underlying problem or cause of the surgery.

I. MATCHING.
Match the correct heading to the definition.

1. ____ This is listed to show the probable diagnosis, rule out a diagnosis, or state an unconfirmed diagnosis prior to the procedure.

2. ____ This lists the diagnosis made after the surgery is performed and the surgeon has had the opportunity to explore the disease body area or organ system thoroughly to pinpoint the problem.

3. ____ A listing of all the surgical procedures in order of priority that were performed on the patient.

4. ____ The physician who performed the surgery.

5. ____ Any physicians who were present and assisted the primary physician with the operation.

6. ____ The type of anesthetic used.

7. ____ The amount of blood lost during the procedure.

8. ____ The background information on why an operation is being performed.

9. ____ An actual description of what occurred during the surgery.

10. ____ The listing of the outcome of the surgery, specifying what was found to be the underlying problem or cause of the surgery.

A. Findings
B. Preoperative Diagnosis
C. Indication for operation
D. Operations
E. Surgeon
F. Assistant Surgeon(s)
G. Postoperative Diagnosis
H. Estimated blood loss
I. Anesthesia
J. Procedure

Unit 7
Physical Examination

Physical Examination – Introduction

The Physical Examination, sometimes called Physical Exam or PE, is an objective evaluation and physical assessment of the body's systems. This is not to be confused with the Review of Systems, which is a subjective review of the body's symptoms. Basically, the physician inspects the body, feels the various parts (palpation), listens to sounds produced by tapping (percussion) and sounds without tapping (auscultation).

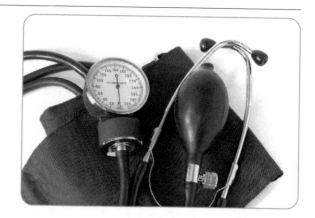

A patient complaining of chest pain might have a longer cardiovascular and/or lung assessment, or perhaps one that is more in depth, during the physical examination. This can occur on an inpatient or outpatient basis, in a clinic or a hospital, so the physical examination is a component that merits an in-depth review as you work your way through this training program.

Elements of the physical exam may include some or all of the following.

- General
    - overall appearance that may include all or some of the following:
    - age
    - race
    - emotional state
    - build of body
    - nutritional state

- Vital Signs
    - temperature
    - blood pressure
    - respiratory rate
    - pulse
    - height
    - weight

- HEENT
    - head
    - eyes
    - ears
    - nose
    - throat

- Neck
- Lungs
- Chest
- Cardiovascular/Heart
- Abdomen
- Genitourinary
- Musculoskeletal/Extremities
- Neurological
- Skin
- Psychiatric

The physical exam is the doctor's objective evaluation of the body and its systems (as opposed to the Review of Systems, which is the *patient's* report of systemic problems). To give you an overview as to how the PE might appear in a medical record, the following is a sample physical examination section of a report:

Physical Examination

PHYSICAL EXAMINATION: When he was first seen in the emergency room he was pale, slightly dyspneic at rest, and otherwise in no acute distress. Vitals: Pulse 120, afebrile, blood pressure 106/40, weight 132 pounds, which is 1 pound less than 1 month ago. Neck: Marked JVD and hepatojugular reflux as before, and again JVD even when standing. Cardiovascular exam: Tachycardia with summation gallop and possible new aortic insufficiency murmur. He still had his very obvious mitral regurgitation. Lungs: Fine basilar rales. Abdomen: Nontender. Liver may be a couple of fingerbreadths below his costal margin but did not percuss large. He did not have any edema. Most significantly, and different from last month, was that his legs demonstrated widespread purpura bilaterally from the midthigh down. Fundi did not reveal any hemorrhage or rough spots. He had no splinter hemorrhages in his extremities.

Sometimes, the subheadings will be stacked—that is, in a vertical fashion atop each other and left justified—and other times (as in this example), they will be in paragraph style. You will see the PE done a variety of ways throughout this unit and the entire training program. Dictator preferences, account specifics, and transcription editing instructions will provide you the direction needed to set this up properly.

Physical Examination Abbreviations

"The patient was AAO until an hour ago when on A&P, some congestion was heard. Family doctor was called, and an EKG was ordered STAT!" Perhaps you've heard those words spoken by a character on one of the many medically themed TV shows airing these days. In reality, these funky sounding words actually have meaning.

An abbreviation is simply a shortened form of a word or a phrase that is used in place of the whole. Abbreviations are prevalent in the world of medicine, and you can expect they will be interspersed throughout the physical examination. It is important for you, as a transcription editor, to have an understanding of what these abbreviations mean. Doctors will often use a shortened form of a word (the abbreviation) to succinctly and quickly convey the medical information they need to have documented in the medical record. Having an understanding of these medical *shortcuts* will assist you greatly in your journey to become a medical transcription editor.

The next time you are watching a medical show on TV, try to decipher some of the abbreviations you hear. Hearing them and seeing the context in which they are used is a fun way to process and learn this information. Doctor's orders!

In the lessons that follow we will review frequently used abbreviations associated with the physical examination. For the most part, abbreviations have more than one translation or meaning, so it is generally best to consult your references for variations when you are working as a medical transcription editor. The abbreviations presented here, however, are all relative to the physical exam.

PE Abbreviations – Lesson 1

I. ENTER ABBREVIATIONS.
Enter the abbreviation and what it stands for.

A&P: auscultation and percussion
Subheading: General, Heart/Cardiovascular

1. _____ (Abbreviation)

2. _____

BP: blood pressure
Subheading: Vital Signs

3. _____ (Abbreviation)

4. _____

CCE: clubbing, cyanosis, or edema
Subheading: Extremities

5. _____ (Abbreviation)

6. _____

CNS: central nervous system
Subheading: Neurology

7. _____ (Abbreviation)

8. _____

CVA: costovertebral angle
Subheading: Abdomen

9. _____ (Abbreviation)

10. _____

RRR: regular rate and rhythm
Subheading: Heart/Cardiovascular

11. _____ (Abbreviation)

12. _____

TMs: tympanic membranes
Subheading: HEENT

13. _____ (Abbreviation)

14. _____

SOM: serous otitis media
Subheading: HEENT

15. _____ (Abbreviation)

16. _____

BUS: Bartholin glands, urethra, and Skene glands
Subheading: OB/GYN

   17. _____ (Abbreviation)

   18. _____

AV: arteriovenous
Subheading: HEENT (AV nicking), Heart/Cardiovascular

   19. _____ (Abbreviation)

   20. _____

II. FILL IN THE BLANK.
Expand the abbreviation for each of the following.

1. CCE _____   2. BUS _____

3. TMs _____   4. A&P _____

5. SOM _____   6. RRR _____

7. BP _____   8. AV _____

9. CNS _____   10. CVA _____

PE Abbreviations – Lesson 2

I. ENTER ABBREVIATIONS.
Enter the abbreviation and what it stands for.

DTRs: deep tendon reflexes
Subheading: Neurological

   1. _____ (Abbreviation)

   2. _____

GI: gastrointestinal
Subheading: GI

   3. _____ (Abbreviation)

   4. _____

EOMs: extraocular movements
Subheading: HEENT

   5. _____ (Abbreviation)

   6. _____

HEENT: head, eyes, ears, nose, throat
Subheading: HEENT

   7. _____ (Abbreviation)

   8. _____

IAC: internal auditory canal
Subheading: HEENT

   9. _____ (Abbreviation)

  10. _____

GU: genitourinary
Subheading: GU

 11. _____ (Abbreviation)

 12. _____

JVD: jugular venous distention
Subheading: Neck

 13. _____ (Abbreviation)

 14. _____

AD: right ear
Subheading: HEENT

 15. _____ (Abbreviation)

 16. _____

AS: left ear
Subheading: HEENT

 17. _____ (Abbreviation)

 18. _____

AU: both ears
Subheading: HEENT

 19. _____ (Abbreviation)

 20. _____

II. MATCHING.
Match the abbreviation with the subheading in which it would be found on a physical exam. Some answers may be used more than once.

1. ____ IAC

2. ____ JVD

3. ____ AD

4. ____ DTRs

5. ____ AU

A. HEENT
B. Neck
C. Cardiovascular
D. Neurological

PE Abbreviations – Lesson 3

I. ENTER ABBREVIATIONS.
Enter the abbreviation and what it stands for.

JVP: jugular venous pressure
Subheading: Neck

1. _____ (Abbreviation)

2. _____

NAD: no acute distress
Subheading: General

3. _____ (Abbreviation)

4. _____

NCAT: normocephalic, atraumatic
Subheading: HEENT

5. _____ (Abbreviation)

6. _____

OD: right eye
Subheading: HEENT

7. _____ (Abbreviation)

8. _____

OS: left eye
Subheading: HEENT

9. _____ (Abbreviation)

10. _____

OU: both eyes
Subheading: HEENT

11. _____ (Abbreviation)

12. _____

TMJ: temporomandibular joint
Subheading: HEENT

13. _____ (Abbreviation)

14. _____

FHT: fetal heart tone
Subheading: OB/GYN, GU

15. _____ (Abbreviation)

16. _____

PVCs: premature ventricular contractions
Subheading: General, Heart/Cardiovascular

17. _____ (Abbreviation)

18. _____

DTs: delirium tremens
Subheading: Neurology/Mental Status

19. _____ (Abbreviation)

20. _____

II. FILL IN THE BLANK.
Enter the appropriate term to complete the expansion of the abbreviation.

1. FHT – fetal _____ tone

2. NCAT – _____, atraumatic

3. TMJ – temporomandibular _____

4. OD – _____ eye

5. NAD – no acute _____

6. DTs – _____ tremens

7. OU – both _____

8. JVP – _____ venous pressure

9. OS – _____ eye

10. PVCs – premature_____ contractions

PE Abbreviations – Lesson 4

I. **ENTER ABBREVIATIONS.**
   Enter the abbreviation and what it stands for.

PERRLA: pupils equal, round, reactive to light and accommodation
Subheading: HEENT

1. _____ (Abbreviation)

2. _____

PMI: point of maximal impulse
Subheading: Heart/Cardiovascular

3. _____ (Abbreviation)

4. _____

REM: rapid eye movement
Subheading: HEENT

5. _____ (Abbreviation)

6. _____

ROM: range of motion
Subheading: Extremities

7. _____ (Abbreviation)

8. _____

LLQ: left lower quadrant
Subheading: Abdomen

9. _____ (Abbreviation)

10. _____

LUQ: left upper quadrant
Subheading: Abdomen

11. _____ (Abbreviation)

12. _____

RLQ: right lower quadrant
Subheading: Abdomen

13. _____ (Abbreviation)

14. _____

AKA: above-knee amputation
Subheading: Extremities

15. _____ (Abbreviation)

16. _____

BKA: below-knee amputation
Subheading: Extremities

17. _____ (Abbreviation)

18. _____

SOB: shortness of breath
Subheading: Lungs

19. _____ (Abbreviation)

20. _____

II. FILL IN THE BLANK.
Enter the appropriate term to complete the expansion of the abbreviation.

1. RLQ – _____ lower quadrant

2. SOB – shortness of _____

3. PERRLA – pupils equal, _____, reactive to light and accommodation

4. BKA – below-knee _____

5. ROM – _____ of motion

6. REM – _____ eye movements

7. PMI – point of _____ impulse

8. AKA – _____ -knee amputation

9. LUQ – left _____ quadrant

10. LLQ – left _____ quadrant

Physical Examination Samples

Now that you have an opportunity to see some of the many abbreviations that dictators use in the Physical Exam portion of a report, take a few minutes to glance over the samples below. These are a small representative sampling of sentences, medical terms, and abbreviations an MTE can expect to see when editing the PE (Physical Examination) section of a report.

Medical Record

Physical Examination

PHYSICAL EXAMINATION: General: On admission, she was a pleasant, elderly female, conversant, alert, looking comfortable and not acutely ill. Skin exam: Crusting on the left pinna and thickened scaly skin with early decubitus changes on the sacrum and ischial spines, as well as both greater tuberosities. HEENT: Her left TM had a dry perforation. Her right TM was okay. Nose was clear. Pupils were small, but reactive with extraocular motions intact. Fundi could not be seen. She had only a few teeth and some black coating on her tongue from nicotine. Neck: There was no jugular venous distention, no neck masses or adenopathy. Chest: Breasts were quite nodular bilaterally, no dominant masses. Lungs: She had wet crackles at both lung bases one third of the way up bilaterally and fine rales up to one half of the way up. Her respiratory rate on admission was 16. Cardiovascular: Heart exam showed a regular rhythm, normal S1 and S2, no S3 or S4, pulse of 84, blood pressure of 124/56. There was no murmur. She had good pulses in all extremities. Abdomen: Obese with no masses or bruits, no tenderness, no organomegaly. The liver edge was sharp, firm, and nontender. Rectal exam: Poor sphincter tone, no rectal masses, and no stool to guaiac test. Extremities: Trace to 1+ edema to the midshins. The skin on the feet was intact. No clubbing, cyanosis, or edema. Neurological: Vibratory sense absent below the knees and light touch absent below the midfoot. Deep tendon reflexes were absent in the lower extremities. Cranial nerves 2-12 were grossly intact. Gait was normal.

Medical Record

Physical Examination

PHYSICAL EXAMINATION: The patient is a quiet, well-developed, well-nourished young girl in no acute distress, but somewhat uncomfortable. Temperature 97.5 axillary, pulse 76, respirations 12, weight 58 pounds. Ears reveal the right ear is slightly erythematous, slightly bulging, good light reflex and landmarks; left is gray, clear. Eyes show clear sclerae, extraocular muscles intact, pupils equal and reactive to light. Fundi show normal disks and vessels. Nose is crusty and clear with blood-tinged discharge, erythema, and chafing below the nares. On mouth exam, the patient is only able to open slightly, mucous membranes moist. Throat reveals erythema, right tonsillar area much greater than left, but both erythematous without exudates. Neck is supple with large 3–4 cm submandibular nodes, 1–2 cm left submandibular node, tender, not stiff, good anterior occipital movement. Lungs with equal movement without retractions, clear to auscultation without rales, rhonchi, or wheezes. Heart has regular rate and rhythm, S1, S2. Abdomen shows good bowel sounds, soft, nontender, no hepatosplenomegaly or masses. Extremities reveals normal muscle strength. Vascular exam shows 2+ pulses. Neurologic is normal. GU is deferred.

Physical Examination

PHYSICAL EXAMINATION: The patient is an alert x3, well-nourished, 41-year-old Caucasian male. Lesions: The only one seen was ulcer, plantar left foot. Hair: Decreased fullness, male pattern baldness, no scalp lesions. Face is symmetrical. Eyes: Equal, extraocular muscles intact. PERRLA, positive reactivity and positive compensation of the eyes. Nose: Septum midline with a patent air flow, no blockage of the nares. Ears had a positive red reflex, no lesions nor inflammation. Mouth: Positive dentures; gingiva was pink, moist, with no bleeding. Uvula was in the midline. Neck: Supple neck, full range of motion, no pain on range of motion, no carotid bruits, positive +2/4 pulses, no jugular vein distention, no thyromegaly, and trachea was in midline. Lymph nodes: No palpable lymph nodes were noted. Back: Full range of motion and no pain on range of motion. Thorax and lungs: Clear to auscultation bilaterally. No rales, rubs, or crackles were noted with 3 cm distention of the diaphragm on inspiration. Heart: Regular rate and rhythm was noted. No murmurs or gallops, no S3 or S4 heart sounds and +2/4 radial pulses. Abdomen: Obese, soft, no palpable masses or tenderness, bowel sounds times 4+. No hernias. Upper extremity had +3/4 tendon reflexes, +4/5 muscle strength, no pain on range of motion, and full range of motion. Lower extremity exam: +2/4 DP and PT pulses bilaterally, capillary fill time was less than 3 seconds to all digits bilaterally, positive hair growth, no edema; and triphasic Doppler pulse, dorsalis pedis, and posterior tibial pulses bilaterally. Ulcer with hyperkeratotic lesion, sub second metatarsal shaft, left foot, no erythema, no odor, no streaking, and the ulcer measured 1 cm in diameter. Musculoskeletal: The patient had +5/5 muscle strength in all four quadrants, +2/4 Achilles tendon reflex, +2/4 patellar reflex, and amputated toes bilaterally. Neurological: The patient had decreased sharp/dull, but had intact proprioception and vibratory sense with no clonus and no Babinski bilaterally.

I. **MULTIPLE CHOICE.**
   Choose the best answer.

1. In the first medical record example, what part of the exam indicated a dry perforation in the left TM?
   - ○ Lungs
   - ○ Neck
   - ○ Abdomen
   - ○ HEENT

2. What does HEENT mean?
   - ○ head, esophagous, eyes, nose, throat
   - ○ head, eyes, ears, nose, throat
   - ○ hearing, eyesight, eating habits, nasal function, throat function
   - ○ head motion, eyesight, ear function, nasal inflamation, throat swelling

3. In the first medical record example, no CCE is present. What is CCE?

○ clubbing, cyanosis, or edema
○ coughing, cracking, or edema
○ clubbing, cracking, or edema
○ coughing, cyanosis, or eating disorder

4. In the second medical record example, what does the abbreviation GU indicate?

○ gastrointestinal
○ genitourinary
○ gastrourinary
○ genitointestinal

5. In the third medical record example, the doctor indicates positive reactivity and positive compensation of the eyes. This is another way of stating what?"

○ HEENT
○ GU
○ PERRLA
○ DP and PT

6. In the third medical record example, the heart is noted to have a _____.

○ RRR: regular rate and rhythm
○ IRR: irregular rate and rhythm
○ R3: regular rate and rhythm
○ RRaR: regular rate and rhythm

Physical Examination Subheadings

As you now know, the Physical Examination (PE) is a summary of the objective findings of the person conducting the actual exam—the examiner/physician. The Physical Exam often consists of subheadings that cover the many body systems observed by the physician. These subheadings tend to follow a specific format, regardless of who you work for or what account you are assigned. So as you work through these subheadings, keep in mind that the order in which the subheadings are presented is generally the customary way they are dictated in the "real world."

Below is an example of a typical Physical Exam portion of a report in which the subheadings are stacked vertically. On the following pages, we will dissect each of these subheadings so that you become familiar with the content and information contained in each.

PHYSICAL EXAMINATION

GENERAL: The patient is a 66-year-old male in no apparent distress. He is alert and oriented x3.

VITAL SIGNS: Temperature 97.7, pulse 60, respirations 20, blood pressure 156/82, and O2 saturation 94% on room air.

HEENT: Head is normocephalic. Extraocular muscles are intact. Pupils are equally round and reactive to light and accommodation. Nares are patent. Mouth reveals very poor dentition. Mucous membranes are moist. Posterior pharynx is without lesions or exudate.

NECK: Supple. No JVD. No carotid bruits. No lymphadenopathy.

LUNGS: Clear to auscultation bilaterally.

CARDIOVASCULAR: Regular rate and rhythm but bradycardic. There is an approximate 2/6 to 3/6 systolic murmur heard along the left sternal border. There is mechanical clicking of S2. The patient has a sternal scar present with keloid formation.

ABDOMEN: Obese, soft, nontender, nondistended. Normoactive bowel sounds. No palpable masses.

EXTREMITIES: No clubbing, cyanosis, or edema. Peripheral pulses are +2 in the upper and lower extremities bilaterally.

NEUROLOGIC: Cranial nerves 2-12 are grossly intact. Strength is 5/5 in the upper and lower extremities bilaterally.

PSYCHIATRIC: Affect is flat. Patient denies suicidal or homicidal ideations.

SKIN: The patient's skin is dry and somewhat scaly.

I. TRUE/FALSE.
Mark the following true or false.

1. The order of the body system subheadings generally follows the same order in the real world.
   - ○ true
   - ○ false

2. JVD, as mentioned under the NECK heading, means jugular venous distention.
   - ○ true
   - ○ false

3. In a physical examination medical record, the HEENT subheading should always be first.

○ true
○ false

4. A note of no CCE is found under the cardiovascular heading.

○ true
○ false

General and Vital Signs

General

The first subheading you will most likely find in the Physical Examination is General. This includes the generalities of the patient's current state. Some of these include appearance, state of alertness, personal hygiene, nutritional status, mood, gait, emotional condition, and even anomalies that can be seen with the naked eye (for example, scars, moles, physical defects, etc.).

GENERAL Exam Examples

- *The patient is a 54-year-old Caucasian female who is well-nourished, well-developed, and presently in no acute distress.*
- *The newborn showed an Apgar score of 7 at one minute and 8 at five minutes.*
- *She appears in no acute distress although mildly cushingoid with masked facies.*
- *He is awake and oriented x3 with no orthostatic changes.*
- *The patient is a 15-year-old, healthy-appearing teenager who is well-developed though slightly obtunded. She is in no acute distress and is responsive, bright, and alert.*

Highlights

Some terms you might hear in the General section: *well-developed, well-nourished, alert and oriented, nontoxic, awake, cyanotic, halitosis, pressured speech, spastic gait, action tremor, productive cough, obese, wasting, oriented to time, place, and person.*

Vital Signs

As you might have guessed, the Vital Signs subheading lists temperature, pulse, respirations, and blood pressure. Sometimes, this information might be given as part of the general examination. These are the quantitative measurements of the patient and are an integral part of the physical examination. Some dictators list the patient's height and weight as well. The temperature might be dictated as Fahrenheit or Celsius. More and more physicians are also expressing patient weight using kilograms (kg), so it is important to properly edit what has been dictated.

VITAL SIGNS Exam Examples

- *The patient's temperature is 98.6, afebrile. Her blood pressure is 124/75, pulse 76 and regular.*
- *He is 5 feet 8 inches, weight 215 pounds. Other vital signs not recorded.*
- *Vital signs are stable, but blood pressure was high this morning at 145/90.*
- *The patient was uncooperative, so blood pressure, pulse, and respiratory rate were unable to be assessed.*
- *Rectal temperature obtained was 101.3, which is a slight increase over the last 24 hours. Blood pressure and pulse remain stable at 120/80 and 75, respectively.*

Highlights

Some terms you might hear in the Vital Signs section are: *fever, afebrile, febrile, labored breathing, apical pulse, labile, hypertensive, hypotensive, pansystolic murmur, unobtainable, rectal temperature, pyrexia.*

I. **MULTIPLE CHOICE.**
   Choose the best answer.

1. Which of the following is NOT an example of a common term in the General section?
   - ○ spastic gait
   - ○ hypotensive
   - ○ obese
   - ○ well-nourished

2. Which of the following is NOT an example of a common term in the Vital Signs section?
   - ○ cyanotic
   - ○ apical pulse
   - ○ labile
   - ○ pyrexia

3. The General subheading typically contains which of the following?

   ○ temperature, weight, blood pressure, height, etc.
   ○ description of the head, ears, eyes, nose and throat
   ○ state of alertness, personal hygiene, appearance, mood, etc.
   ○ The date, location, and name of the patient

4. Which of the following is an example of what you might find under the Vital Signs subheading?

   ○ Patient is 54 years old, presenting a productive cough.
   ○ Muscle tone is good.
   ○ Abdomen is obese, soft, nontender, nondistended.
   ○ Patient is 5 feet 6 inches, 175 pounds. Her blood pressure is 124/75.

HEENT

The General and Vital Signs subheadings are typically followed by HEENT, which translates to head, ears, eyes, nose, and throat. If the skin exam is a part of this, it may be referred to as SHEENT. Each of these subtopics are then examined and dictated. For our purposes, we will cover contents under each individual letter in HEENT. Let's break it down!

HEAD: Size and shape of the skull, color and texture of skin and hair, facial structure and features, scarring or defects of the head and face, jaw and mouth movement. These are but a few of the many things assessed in exam of the head. Teeth may also be assessed as part of the head exam.

EARS: The tympanic membranes, canals, ossicles, bones, hearing, balance (equilibrium), and physical anomalies are all examined as a part of the ear examination. Expect to hear abbreviations (which were covered in the previous section) such as AD (right ear), AS (left ear), and AU (both ears).

EYES: Examination of the sclerae, corneas, conjunctivae, EOMs (extraocular movements), visual acuity, visual fields, eye chambers, pupils (often edited as PERRLA), color vision, fundi, and/or with more in-depth assessment and testing if done by an ophthalmologist.

NOSE: The airway, sinuses, nasal septum, and sense of smell are all considerations in this assessment.

Highlights

Some words you might hear in a HEENT examination are:

HEAD: *normocephalic, atraumatic, symmetrical, occiput, alopecia, masked facies, microcephaly, sagittal suture, allergic shiners, facial edema, jaundice.*
EARS: *acoustic meatus, ear canal, eardrum, tympanic membranes, Valsalva maneuver, otitis media, otorrhea, exudate, cerumen, vertigo.*
EYES: *sclerae, dilated pupils, keratitis, globe, ectropion, orbital rim, palpebral fissures, scotoma, accommodation, fundi, intraocular pressure, iritis, anterior segment, corneal ulcer, nystagmus.*
NOSE: *patent nares, rhinorrhea, epistaxis, middle meatus, mucous membrane, boggy turbinates, nasolabial fold, polyps, congestion, sinuses, flattening, hypertrophy.*
THROAT: *tonsillar fossa, gag reflex, tonsillar crypts, erythema, exudates, edentulous, thrush, tongue is midline, cleft palate, phonation.*

THROAT: If the mouth has not been assessed as part of the head exam, the examiner will often include it as part of the throat assessment. Teeth, lips, gums, tongue, salivary glands, hard and soft palate, uvula, and oral mucosa are all a part of this. Oral cavity inspection is done with the aid of a tongue depressor and light. Pharynx is viewed when the patient says "ahhh" and allows for a closer look. Any lesions, growth, discharge, hemorrhage, or exudates are noted. In addition, the odor of the breath is assessed, as many diseases and conditions are associated with foul or abnormal breath.

- *HEAD: Head is atraumatic, normocephalic.*
- *EYES: Pupils are equal, round, and reactive to light and accommodation. EOMs intact.*
- *EARS: Hearing and eardrums are intact.*
- *NOSE: Flattening of the nasolabial fold is present, but otherwise no abnormalities detected.*
- *THROAT: Upon testing of gag reflex, uvula projects upward.*
- *HEENT: Pupils equal, round, and reactive to light. Extraocular movements are full. Nose soft without lesions. Dentition is in adequate condition.*
- *HEENT: Head examination, normocephalic. Positive vitiligo on the right side of the face. Funduscopy normal. No papilledema. No retinal changes. Nose and throat are clear. Ear examination is normal. Throat examination, no signs of infection.*
- *HEENT showed no head trauma. TMs were normal bilaterally with scarring. Pupils were equal, round, and reactive to light. Extraocular motions were intact with no injection. Nares were clear but reddened. The throat was not red, with no exudate. Tongue was tobacco stained. Teeth were in fair repair.*

I. FILL IN THE BLANK.
Enter the correct word in the blank provided.

1. Any scarring or defects of the face would be included under this subheading.

   _____

2. A deviated nasal septum would be indicated under this subheading. _____

3. EOM and PERRLA would be examples of information found under this subheading.

   _____

4. An assessment of balance and tympanic membranes would be found under this subheading.

   _____

5. The gag reflex and odor of the breath are assessed under this subheading. _____

Neck, Lungs, and Chest

Neck

If not included in the HEENT exam, the neck exam will be dictated separately. Information in this area includes neck mobility, contour, shape, assessment of lymph nodes, tracheal position, distention of neck veins, carotid pulses, limitations on movement, masses, growths, swelling, thyroid gland assessment.

NECK Exam Examples

- *Neck is supple with no masses present. Trachea deviates slightly to the right.*
- *Carotid pulsations are equal and slight bruit is present. No neck vein distention.*
- *Supple with no evidence of jugular venous distention.*
- *JVD is noted with 3+ distention. No rigidity but parotid gland on the right is noted to be enlarged.*
- *Shotty lymph nodes and slight enlargement of thyroid gland. Masses are not present.*

Lungs

In a lung exam, the examiner is listening to breath sounds, lung fields, and the patient is usually seated. A&P are the key methods used in this exam portion and these stand for auscultation (listening) and percussion (tapping). Inhalation and exhalation are performed in order to assess the lungs.

LUNG Exam Examples

- *Clear to auscultation and percussion.*
- *Fine basilar rales noted.*
- *Lungs showed a thoracotomy over the left lower chest. He had marked bronchial breath sounds in the left upper chest both anteriorly and posteriorly, with a few crackles in the left midchest. The rest of the lungs were clear.*
- *An end-expiratory wheeze was found of the right lung. Left lung showed no signs of abnormality.*

Chest

Sometimes a grouping separate from the lung exam will be performed that concentrates on the chest, breasts, and/or axillae areas. In this case, the size, shape, and symmetry of the breasts is more closely assessed. Breathing movement can also be viewed during this time as part of the overall chest wall examination. Sometimes the thorax and lung examinations are combined.

Highlights

Some terms you might hear in the Chest/Breasts/Axillae section are: *areola, atrophic, mastectomy, thoracic, costal margins, intercostal spaces, barrel chest, midclavicular line, gynecomastia, pectus excavatum, axillary line, peau d'orange, costochondritis, lymphadenopathy.*

Cardiovascular, Abdomen, and GU

Cardiovascular/Heart

The heart is auscultated in order to listen for the rhythm, rubs, gallops, heaves, or murmurs. The circulatory system affects all of the body's other systems, so if the heart has an abnormality, it may manifest itself in the eye exam, the neck exam, and so on. Since the examiner usually has the patient seated and has just performed the lung and/or chest exam, often the cardiac portion of the physical examination is next.

CARDIOVASCULAR Exam Examples

- *S1, S2 regular rate and rhythm without murmur, gallop, or rub. PMI is not displaced.*
- *Heart rhythm was basically regular with occasional skipped beats, no murmur.*
- *Regular rate and rhythm with a 2/4 systolic murmur.*
- *Heart exam showed a regular rhythm, normal S1 and S2, no S3 or S4, pulse of 84, blood pressure of 124/56. There was no murmur. She had good pulses in all extremities.*
- *Regular rate and rhythm with a normal S1 and a normal S2, positive S4, grade 1/6 ejection murmur at the left upper sternal border, no elevated JVD or carotid bruits.*

Highlights

Some terms you might hear in the Cardiovascular/Heart section are: *regurgitation, murmurs, gallops, rubs, clicks, thrills, heaves, bradycardia, tachycardia, precordium, flutter, diastolic, systolic, irregularly irregular, PMI (point of maximal impulse), second heart sound.*

Abdomen

The examiner will inspect, auscultate, palpate, and percuss the abdominal area during this portion of the exam. Some physicians will incorporate the groin, rectal, anus, and genitalia exams into this portion as well. Things noted during this exam are the shape, contour, bowel sounds, and palpation of the liver, kidneys, and spleen. By palpating, muscle tone and skin turgor (tension) can be assessed.

ABDOMEN Exam Examples

- *Abdomen showed a recent left abdominal surgical scar, healing well without evidence of infection. She had high-pitched bowel sounds and mild diffuse tenderness, especially in the center of the abdomen. However, the abdomen was soft without distention. Rectal exam showed guaiac negative stool.*
- *Abdomen showed extensive scarring, scaphoid appearance, no masses or organomegaly, no tenderness, and normoactive bowel sounds. Rectal exam showed no masses, guaiac negative stool, and a small, nontender prostate.*
- *Soft with active bowel sounds, no hepatosplenomegaly.*
- *Sigmoid colon is palpable and nontender. Liver span is 9 cm. A spleen tip is palpable.*
- *Obese with no masses or bruits, no tenderness, no organomegaly. The liver edge was sharp, firm, and nontender. Rectal exam: Showed poor sphincter tone, no rectal masses, and no stool to guaiac test.*

Genitourinary

The genitourinary (GU) exam is one that assesses the reproductive organs and the urinary system. A more detailed exam might be performed in the obstetrics/gynecologic setting. In the female exam, this would include the external genitalia, female glands, vagina, cervix, meatus, perineum, and anus. In the male exam, this would include the prostate, testes, and penis.

GU Exam Examples

- *Normal circumcised male phallus with bilaterally descended testes, Foley catheter in place. Digital rectal exam deferred secondary to probable prostatitis.*
- *No history of bladder stones or kidney infections. She has tenderness over the right flank upon palpation.*
- *No penile lesions are detected.*
- *A small uterus is noted with a uterine filling defect. Vaginal discharge detected.*
- *Reducible hernia found on palpation. Descended testicles, no sign of epididymitis.*

I. MULTIPLE CHOICE.
Choose the best answer.

1. ($\bigcirc$Systolic, $\bigcirc$Fluid wave) would be indicated under the Abdomen subheading.

2. ($\bigcirc$Hepatomegaly, $\bigcirc$Heaves) would be indicated under the Cardiovascular/Heart subheading.

3. ($\bigcirc$Perineal, $\bigcirc$Scaphoid) would be indicated under the Genitourinary subheading.

4. Sometimes the groin, rectal, anus, and genitalia exams are included under the ($\bigcirc$ Cardiovascular/Heart, $\bigcirc$Abdomen) subheading.

5. Regurgitation is a term you would most likely hear under ($\bigcirc$Cardiovascular/Heart, $\bigcirc$ Abdomen).

Musculoskeletal

The Physical Examination Musculoskeletal portion is an assessment of the muscles, bones, and joints of the body. Sometimes, the examiner will incorporate the back and/or extremities as part of this examination. A review of the movement is performed as well as inspection of hands, feet, and skin.

If not assessed and examined in the musculoskeletal section, some examiners will choose to identify the extremities on their own in the physical examination. This subheading is aptly titled EXTREMITIES.

MUSCULOSKELETAL/EXTREMITIES Exam Examples

- *Left knee: There is a well-healed midline scar, active range of motion 0 to 90 degrees, a mild amount of effusion, crepitus with patellar grind. The MCL (medial collateral ligament) and LCL (lateral collateral ligament) are intact with varus and valgus stressing, negative tibial sag, negative Lachman's.*
- *There is an area of edema over the posterior talofibular ligament with mild crepitus.*
- *Right knee: Well healed surgical scar, 5 degrees to 90 degrees active range of motion. Left knee: Active range of motion 0 to 130 degrees, 2+ pseudolaxity medially, negative effusion, positive patellar grind, varus malalignment, Lachman, negative pivot, tender medial joint line. Knee score, 60 degrees. Functional score, 50 degrees.*
- *Range of motion of all extremities is within normal limits.*
- *Normal examination. Pulses are 2+/4+ in the dorsalis pedis and posterior tibial.*
- *Palpation of the back reveals normal paraspinous muscle group with slight tenderness over C4.*
- *Range of motion in the hips is limited. There is a 2+ dorsalis pedis pulse on the left, and remaining peripheral pulses are absent.*
- *Range of motion is within normal limits. No evidence of venous disease or arterial disease is found.*
- *Extremities showed good pulses and perfusion. Ortolani and Barlow maneuvers were intact.*
- *The patient had +5/5 muscle strength in all 4 quadrants, +2/4 Achilles tendon reflex, +2/4 patellar reflex, and amputated toes bilaterally.*

I. MULTIPLE CHOICE.
Choose the best answer.

1. BKA stands for _____.
   - ○ below-kidney artery
   - ○ below-knee amputation
   - ○ bulbous kyphosis atrophy
   - ○ below-knee artery

2. The musculoskeletal portion of the Physical Examination is an assessment of _____.
   - ○ only the muscles of the body
   - ○ only the bones of the body
   - ○ only the joints of the body
   - ○ muscles, bones, and joints of the body

3. Which of the following is an example of something you might find under a Musculoskeletal heading?
   - ○ Palpation of the back reveals normal paraspinous muscle group with slight tenderness over C4.
   - ○ Regular rate and rhythm with a 2/4 systolic murmur.
   - ○ Carotid pulsations are equal and slight bruit is present.
   - ○ Clear to auscultation bilaterally. No rales, rubs, crackles were noted with 3 cm distention of the diaphragm on inspiration.

Neurologic and Psychiatric

Neurologic

As part of the Neurological portion of the Physical Exam, tested items will include reflexes; cranial nerves (2–12); orientation to time, place, and person (spheres); patient gait and station, and a series of signs (for example, Babinski, Romberg, Hoffmann). The patient must cooperate for a majority of these tests, as this is an examination and assessment of both the central and peripheral nervous systems.

NEUROLOGIC Exam Examples

- *Cranial nerves 2–12 appear intact. There are no deficits noted.*
- *Coordination unable to be tested. Left-sided tremor is noted consistent with previous diagnosis of Parkinson disease.*
- *Cranial nerves: The patient had no gross field cuts but had difficulty cooperating with his fundus examination. Extraocular muscles intact. Pupils equal, round, reactive to light. Masseter is strong bilaterally. No facial asymmetry. Hearing intact grossly. Palate symmetrical bilaterally. Sternocleidomastoid and trapezoid normal. Tongue midline. Motor: 5/5 strength in all extremities proximally and distally. Tone normal x4 extremities. No abnormal movements nor atrophy. Sensory: Intact to light touch and pinprick. Deep tendon reflexes: 2+ bilateral upper extremities, biceps, triceps, brachioradialis, 3+ knee jerks bilaterally, 1+ ankle jerks bilaterally, toes equivocal. Gait: Normal. Motor coordination and heel-to-shin grossly intact.*
- *Cranial nerves 2–12 grossly intact. Deep tendon reflexes of the biceps, triceps, and brachioradialis 2/4 bilaterally, patellar and Achilles 1+/4 bilaterally. Sensation intact in all extremities. Some hyperesthesias over left palmar surface of hand. Cerebellar, finger-to-nose good with left greater than right. Gait normal. The patient exhibits good balance. Negative Romberg.*
- *Cranial nerves 2–12 are grossly intact. His strength is 5/5 throughout. His deep tendon reflexes are symmetrical with his plantar extension reflex downgoing. There is no clonus. Pinprick and light touch are both normal. His cerebellar function is intact, showing that positive finger-to-nose, heel-to-shin, rapid alternating movements are all intact. He does not have a Romberg sign. He has a slightly unsteady tandem gait and a good heel-to-toe walk.*
- *Cranial nerves 2–12 are intact. Cranial 1 not tested. Cerebellar function within normal limits. Plantar reflexes are down. Deep tendon reflexes at the knee are 2+/4 and at Achilles are 2+/4.*

Psychiatric

Often called the *mental status examination*, this portion of the PE (Physical Exam) is sometimes combined with the neurological exam or is dictated separately. This portion assesses a patient's cognitive (knowledge) ability, appearance, mood, speech, and patterns of thought. Noted will be the patient's level of cooperation and attitude along with the ability or lack thereof, whether by choice or not, to answer questions. Often, this section is more detailed when dictated by an examiner affiliated with the psychiatric department of the facility.

One of the sections you can expect to encounter quite often in a psychiatric assessment is that of the DSM-IV, which is the Diagnostic and Statistical Manual of Mental Disorders. Simply stated, this breaks down the patient's assessment by axes as follows:

Axis I: Clinical disorders and syndromes
Axis II: Personality disorders (including mental retardation)
Axis III: Medical conditions (which can impact mood and emotions)
Axis IV: Psychosocial stressors (death, divorce, job loss, etc.)
Axis V: Global assessment of functioning

PSYCHIATRIC/MENTAL STATUS Exam Examples

- *The patient is a cooperative, pleasant, 53-year-old female who appears in no acute distress. Speech is rapid and mood is described as "sad." Affect is flat. She denies suicidal or homicidal ideations at the present time. She is able to perform serial 7's without difficulty. Able to name three Presidents.*

- *The patient appears older than his stated age of 43. Speech is incoherent, and the examiner was unable to assess the mental status completely due to inability of patient to cooperate.*

- *Mental Status Examination: See admission notes, and discharge diagnoses are given below.*
  - *Axis I: Schizoaffective disorder, bipolar type.*
  - *Axis II: None.*
  - *Axis III: Diabetes mellitus, congestive heart failure, rheumatoid arthritis.*
  - *Axis IV: None.*
  - *Axis V: Global Assessment of Functioning (GAF) on discharge is 45.*

- *The patient is hostile and insisting he wants to go home. He states he has been "drinking a pint a day" for 48 years. He is quite adamant about wanting to leave. Four-point restraints were used and the patient refused to talk further.*

I. FILL IN THE BLANK.
Using the word/word parts in the box, fill in the blanks.

1. A term you might hear in the neurological section is

   _____.

2. A term you might hear in the psychiatric section is

   _____.

3. "Cranial nerves 2-12 are grossly intact" is an example of the

   _____ portion of the Physical Exam.

4. "Speech is rapid and mood is described as sad" is an example of

   the _____ portion of the Physical Exam.

| tangential |
| psychiatric |
| nystagmus |
| neurologic |

Review: Physical Examination Subheadings

I. SPELLING.
Determine if the following words are spelled correctly. If the spelling is correct, leave the word as it has already been entered. If the spelling is incorrect, provide the correct spelling.

1. trachia midline _____

2. nontender _____

3. gauiac _____

4. clonis _____

5. carotid bruitts _____

6. asymetric _____

7. Romberg _____

8. posterior tibial _____

9. plantar _____

10. homocidal ideation _____

II. MULTIPLE CHOICE.
Choose the best answer.

1. The subheading that covers generalities of the patient's current state is (◯Vital Signs, ◯ General).

2. The thyroid gland is assessed in the (◯Chest, ◯Neck) exam.

3. The Vital Signs subheading does not typically report the patient's (◯age, ◯temperature).

4. Range of motion is typically assessed in the (◯Musculoskeletal, ◯Chest) exam.

5. EOMs refer to the (◯eyes, ◯extremities).

6. Murmurs, rubs, and gallops are recorded in the (◯Lung, ◯Cardiovascular) exam.

7. JVD is assessed in the (◯Neck, ◯Cardiovascular) exam.

8. PERRLA is found on the (◯HEENT, ◯Abdominal) exam.

9. Lungs are usually clear to auscultation and (◯palpation, ◯percussion).

10. The term meaning no elevated temperature is (◯febrile, ◯afebrile).

Unit 8
Laboratory Data

Laboratory Data – Introduction

The laboratory data component of a medical report contains the results of lab tests that have been performed on a patient, usually to aid in confirming diagnoses, determining underlying health issues, and monitoring for such conditions as anemia, hypercholesterolemia, hyperglycemia, and electrolyte imbalances. There are many instances where lab studies are the only method to determine the etiology of patient symptoms. For instance, a patient may have feelings of lethargy and confusion with no other obvious physical symptoms. In this case, a CBC may reveal a low hemoglobin, and further iron studies may indicate that the patient is anemic. A physician might suspect anemia but could not confirm this diagnosis without the benefit of being able to perform these lab studies.

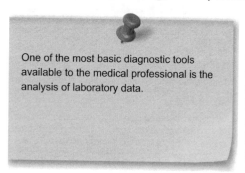

One of the most basic diagnostic tools available to the medical professional is the analysis of laboratory data.

Laboratory tests are often performed upon admission to the hospital or during checkup and followup visits to a physician's office. These laboratory values are extremely important because they provide information that can help establish or rule out diagnoses, such as anemia, diabetes, and kidney failure. Laboratory tests also allow the physician to monitor blood levels for certain medications, such as Coumadin and digoxin levels, which helps in adjusting medications to ensure the wellbeing of the patient. And finally, lab tests called toxicology screens are performed to determine the presence of drugs or poisons both in living patients and in postmortem examinations.

It is important for the working medical transcription editor to thoroughly understand laboratory data and normal values because the results of laboratory studies are frequently cited in medical reports. The amount of laboratory data will vary from one report to another, depending upon the number and severity of a patient's medical problems. Sometimes a physician will dictate all laboratory values for any studies done; other times he/she will only dictate the abnormal values.

You are exposed to laboratory studies in several modules throughout this training program, and by the time you finish the entire training program you will have had very extensive exposure and education on laboratory data as it appears in the context of medical reports. The purpose of this unit is to provide detailed instruction on laboratory data, including laboratory abbreviations, basic laboratory studies, laboratory data in reports, and normal laboratory values.

Laboratory tests are vital to patient care, and correctly edited laboratory test results are equally as important. Fortunately there are a plethora of laboratory references out there (online and hard copy) to help you verify the laboratory data in medical reports!

Understanding Laboratory Data

The laboratory data portion of a medical report is a presentation of the results of diagnostic tests performed on the patient. Laboratory tests analyze the components of substances such as:

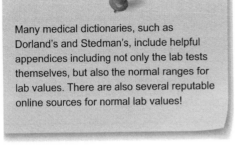

Many medical dictionaries, such as Dorland's and Stedman's, include helpful appendices including not only the lab tests themselves, but also the normal ranges for lab values. There are also several reputable online sources for normal lab values!

- blood
- serum
- urine
- stool
- sputum
- cerebrospinal fluid
- various other fluids
- expired air

Most medical text documents refer to these laboratory results often by their abbreviated, usually acronymic, forms, as you will observe in the samples throughout this unit and the training program.

Again, the lab data material covered in this unit is meant to be a comprehensive overview of the laboratory data you will be exposed to as a medical transcription editor. Diagnostic studies, in general, often include the results of x-rays, electrocardiograms, and other such procedures, as well as chemistry study results. Only the chemistry studies will be considered in this unit.

Without further ado, let's have a look at common laboratory abbreviations.

Laboratory Abbreviations

Many laboratory tests are referred to almost exclusively by their abbreviations. You will generally be required to expand abbreviations in many reports. However, even accounts that require expansion of abbreviations as a default do not necessarily require expanding the standard laboratory abbreviations. It is important, of course, that abbreviations be typed with the correct letters (ABG and not AGG, for example). It is also helpful to know what the abbreviations mean, as this understanding helps in distinguishing the letters as they are spoken.

In a medical report, you will typically find the laboratory data information in a paragraph following the Physical Examination section, although sometimes this information is given as part of the actual Physical Exam itself. Depending on the tests ordered by the treating physician(s), the results will appear in the section under the Laboratory Data heading. Of course, just as the tests ordered vary, so too will the results. In order for you to have a better understanding of laboratory data, the material contained in the following lessons will give you a better understanding of laboratory abbreviations.

By learning these abbreviations now, you will have a better understanding of what the lab tests mean, and eventually you will be able to recognize values which are normal and abnormal. It is called scaffolding—building new knowledge on top of knowledge you already have.

Laboratory Abbreviations – Lesson 1

I. **ENTER ABBREVIATIONS.**
   Enter the abbreviation and what it stands for.

ABG: arterial blood gas
ABGs showed a pH of 7.32, a pCO2 of 24, and a saturation of 93%.

  1. _____ (Abbreviation)

  2. _____

AFB: acid-fast bacillus
The tuberculosis pathogen is an AFB.

  3. _____ (Abbreviation)

  4. _____

BUN: blood urea nitrogen
BUN 12, creatinine 1.6.

  5. _____ (Abbreviation)

  6. _____

CBC: complete blood count
CBC revealed a WBC of 11.6, platelets of 160,000.

  7. _____ (Abbreviation)

  8. _____

CO2: carbon dioxide
Sodium 23, CO2 29, potassium 3.8.

  9. _____ (Abbreviation)

  10. _____

C&S*: culture and sensitivity
C&S was no growth.

  11. _____ (Abbreviation)

  12. _____

Note similarity to CNS. Both sound the same when pronounced aloud.

II. FILL IN THE BLANK.
Using the word/word parts in the box, fill in the blanks.

1. Carbon _____ was 13.

2. Creatinine was 1.2 and blood _____ nitrogen was 11.8.

3. A complete blood _____ was drawn and was within normal limits.

4. _____ blood gas revealed a pH of 7.33.

5. Culture and _____ was done.

6. Acid-fast _____ was negative.

arterial
bacillus
count
dioxide
sensitivity
urea

III. MULTIPLE CHOICE.
Choose the correct term for the abbreviation expansion.

1. CO2 – (◯common, ◯carbon) dioxide

2. C&S – (◯culture, ◯coulture) and sensitivity

3. ABG – (◯arterial, ◯artery) blood gas

4. CBC – complete blood (◯culture, ◯count)

5. BUN – blood (◯urine, ◯urea) nitrogen

Laboratory Abbreviations – Lesson 2

I. ENTER ABBREVIATIONS.
Enter the abbreviation and what it stands for.

CSF: cerebrospinal fluid
CSF was drawn and was within normal limits.

1. _____ (Abbreviation)

2. _____

FEV: forced expiratory volume
The FEV was checked with spirometry.

3. _____ (Abbreviation)

4. _____

FVC: forced vital capacity
The FVC was also checked with spirometry.

5. _____ (Abbreviation)

6. _____

H&H: hemoglobin and hematocrit
CBC showed an H&H of 12.7 and 38.4.

7. _____ (Abbreviation)

8. _____

HIV: human immunodeficiency virus
Labs revealed HIV negative.

9. _____ (Abbreviation)

10. _____

KCl: potassium chloride
Kay Ciel is a trademark for a preparation of KCl.

11. _____ (Abbreviation)

12. _____

LFT: liver function test
His LFTs were grossly abnormal.

13. _____ (Abbreviation)

14. _____

II. **FILL IN THE BLANK.**
   Enter the correct word in the blank provided.

1. His liver _____ tests were within normal limits.

2. CBC showed a _____ and hematocrit of 12.7 and 37.9.

3. She is human _____ virus negative.

4. Her _____ fluid was drawn and was within normal limits.

| cerebrospinal |
| function |
| hemoglobin |
| immunodeficiency |

III. **MULTIPLE CHOICE.**
    Choose the correct term for the abbreviation expansion.

1. H&H – (◯humaglobin, ◯hemoglobin) and hematocrit

2. CSF – (◯cerebrospinal, ◯cerebral) fluid

3. HIV – human (◯immunodeficiency, ◯immunological) virus

4. LFT – (◯living, ◯liver) function test

Laboratory Abbreviations – Lesson 3

I. **ENTER ABBREVIATIONS.**
   Enter the abbreviation and what it stands for.

LP: lumbar puncture
An LP was drawn and was noncontributory.

1. _____ (Abbreviation)

2. _____

O&P: ova and parasites
Stool sample was taken for O&P.

3. _____ (Abbreviation)

4. _____

PFT: pulmonary function test
After nebulizers, PFTs were taken.

5. _____ (Abbreviation)

6. _____

PSA: prostate-specific antigen
All his diagnostic data, including the PSA, indicated no recurrent disease.

7. _____ (Abbreviation)

8. _____

PT: prothrombin time
PT and PTT were normal.

9. _____ (Abbreviation)

10. _____

PTT: partial thromboplastin time
PT and PTT were normal.

11. _____ (Abbreviation)

12. _____

II. FILL IN THE BLANK.
Enter the correct word in the blank provided.

1. Her _____ time was normal.

2. She had an abnormal partial _____ time.

3. _____ puncture was normal.

4. _____ and parasites were negative.

5. Her pulmonary _____ tests were normal.

6. Prostate-specific _____ is a test for prostate cancer.

antigen
function
lumbar
ova
prothrombin
thromboplastin

III. MULTIPLE CHOICE.
Choose the correct term for the abbreviation expansion.

1. O&P – (◯ovary, ◯ova) and parasites

2. PFT – pulmonary (◯failure, ◯function) test

3. PTT – (◯pulmonary, ◯partial) thromboplastin time

4. PT – prothrombin (◯test, ◯time)

5. PSA – prostate-specific (◯antigen, ◯antibody)

Laboratory Abbreviations – Lesson 4

I. ENTER ABBREVIATIONS.
Enter the abbreviation and what it stands for.

RBC/rbc: red blood count/red blood cell
UA was negative for RBCs.

1. _____ (Abbreviation)

2. _____

RPR: rapid plasma reagin
RPR was nonreactive.

3. _____ (Abbreviation)

4. _____

SMA: panel of laboratory tests
His SMA 7 was within normal limits.

5. _____ (Abbreviation)

6. _____

TB: tuberculosis
She had a positive TB test in 1973.

7. _____ (Abbreviation)

8. _____

UA: urinalysis
She had a negative UA.

9. _____ (Abbreviation)

10. _____

WBC/wbc: white blood count/white blood cell
CBC showed WBC 14,000, RBC 5.

11. _____ (Abbreviation)

12. _____

II. FILL IN THE BLANK.
Enter the correct word in the blank provided.

1. Her urinalysis showed no white_____ cells.

2. She had a positive_____ test in the past.

3. She had no evidence of red blood_____ in the urine.

4. She had a negative clean catch_____.

blood
cells
tuberculosis
urinalysis

III. MULTIPLE CHOICE.
Choose the correct term for the abbreviation expansion.

1. UA – (◯urinalysis, ◯uric acid)

2. RBC – (◯real, ◯red) blood count

3. WBC – (◯white, ◯wasted) blood count

4. TB – (◯total body, ◯tuberculosis)

Basic Laboratory Studies – Lesson 1

With the laboratory abbreviations under your belt, it is time to take a look at basic lab studies. This overview of lab studies will help you put the lab abbreviations into context. Although it is not meant to be a comprehensive study of **all** laboratory tests performed, approximately 90% of the laboratory studies you will encounter as a working MTE are covered here.

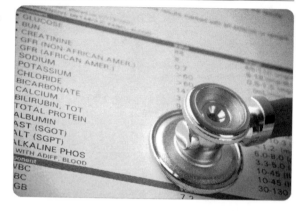

Arterial Blood Gas Study/ABG

ABGs are performed in order to test oxygen function in the lungs and how well carbon dioxide is expelled from the bloodstream. Blood is drawn from an artery and values include: pH (test for acid/alkaline base), PaO2 (oxygenation pressure measurement), PaCO2 (carbon dioxide dissolution assessment), HCO3 (bicarbonate), and SaO2 (oxygen saturation levels).

- The arterial blood gas studies are used to determine pulmonary function in patients with asthma, pneumonia, acute respiratory distress syndrome, and other respiratory ailments.
- Often included in the review of ABGs is the oxygen saturation in the blood (determined by pulse oximetry). This is presented as a percentage, with preferred values being in the mid to high 90s.

Basic Metabolic Panel/BMP

The BMP includes values for the following: Sodium, potassium, chloride, CO2, BUN (blood urea nitrogen), creatinine, glucose, calcium.

- A physician may order a BMP in order to monitor such things as electrolyte balances, kidney status, blood sugar, and calcium levels. Significant changes in these values can indicate acute problems, such as kidney failure, diabetic problems, respiratory distress, heart rhythm changes, or seizure.
- The BMP may be referred to as Chem-7 or SMA-7, although technically they are different. The BMP contains the Chem-7 values, plus one more electrolyte value. SMA is an abbreviation derived from the equipment that processes lab samples (simultaneous multichannel autoanalyzer).

Beta HCG (human chorionic gonadotropin)

Test to determine the level of pregnancy hormones (pregnancy tests).

Cardiac Studies

CK (creatine kinase), CPK (creatine phosphokinase), CPK-MB (myocardial band enzymes of CPK), troponins.

Cardiac studies are used to determine the presence of cardiac biomarkers (enzymes, hormones, or proteins) that would indicate heart damage from events such as myocardial infarctions or coronary thromboses.

Cerebrospinal Fluid/CSF

Protein, glucose, cells.

Analysis of CSF may provide information leading to diagnosis of such conditions as trauma, meningitis, and polyneuritis. CSF is obtained by means of a lumbar puncture (LP), and the lab report may specify LP rather than CSF.

Coagulation Studies

PT/INR (prothrombin time/international normalized ratio) and PTT (partial thromboplastin time).

Coagulation studies determine the time it takes for blood to clot, and abnormal values could indicate risks for excessive bleeding or stroke. Other less common coagulation studies are done, as well.

Complete Blood Count/CBC

Leukocytes (white blood cells), hemoglobin, hematocrit, platelets, red blood cells (rbc's), MCV (mean corpuscular volume) and MCH (mean corpuscular hemoglobin), MCHC (mean corpuscular hemoglobin concentration), erythrocyte sedimentation rate (most often dictated as "sed rate").

The CBC measures different blood components that may indicate underlying health issues. For instance, the hemoglobin value tells how much oxygen is inside your blood cells, hematocrit details the volume of space your blood is occupying, and platelet counts determine the clotting ability of your blood. A high white blood cell count could indicate infection.

Several types of leukocytes are identified: Myelocytes, band neutrophils (bands), segmented neutrophils (segs), lymphocytes, monocytes, eosinophils, basophils, granulocytes. The ratio of these wbc's to one another—as percentages—is called "the differential" on a CBC; the components of the differential should always add up to 100%, (although all the components may not always be dictated).

RBC can refer to either red blood count or red blood cell; WBC can refer to either white blood count or white blood cell. In lower case (rbc/wbc), the reference is nearly always to cell, not count.

Comprehensive Metabolic Panel/CMP

Electrolytes, glucose, BUN, creatinine, albumin, total bilirubin, calcium, alkaline phosphatase (ALP), total protein (TP), AST (serum aspartate aminotransferase), ALT (alanine aminotransferase).

Notice that the comprehensive panel includes electrolytes, kidney function studies, and liver function studies, as well as glucose (blood sugar).

I. **MULTIPLE CHOICE.**
   Choose the best answer.

1. A CBC is a test to determine levels of _____.
   - ○ electrolytes and creatinine
   - ○ protein and glucose
   - ○ human chorionic gonadotropin
   - ○ hemoglobin and platelets

2. If you wanted to determine if you were pregnant, you would take this test.
   - ○ Beta HCG
   - ○ BMP
   - ○ CSF
   - ○ CMP

3. This type of test includes values for pH, FEV, FVC, O2 and CO2.
   - ○ BMP
   - ○ ABG
   - ○ Cardiac Studies
   - ○ Coagulation Studies

4. This tests for CK, CPK, CPK-MB, and troponins.
   - ○ BMP
   - ○ ABG
   - ○ Cardiac Studies
   - ○ Coagulation Studies

5. Coagulation studies determine _____.
   - ○ the time it takes for blood to clot
   - ○ the amount of oxygen inside your blood cells
   - ○ a diagnosis of trauma, meningitis, and polyneritis
   - ○ blood sugar levels

6. If you wanted to find levels of bilirubin, calcium, and creatinine, you would use this test.
   - ○ BMP
   - ○ CMP
   - ○ CBC
   - ○ CSF

7. CSF is obtained by means of _____.
   - ○ LP (lumbar puncture)
   - ○ a blood test
   - ○ urinalysis
   - ○ testing saliva

8. A BMP includes values for what?
   - ○ hemoglobin, hematocrit, platelets, and red blood cells
   - ○ sodium, potassium, BUN, glucose, and calcium
   - ○ electrolytes, BUN, calcium, total protein, and albumin
   - ○ pH, FEV, FVC, O2, CO2

Basic Laboratory Studies – Lesson 2

Chem-7

Glucose, BUN, creatinine, CO2, chloride, potassium, and sodium

Electrolytes (Often Referred To As "lytes")

Sodium (Na), potassium (K), chloride (Cl), and bicarbonate or bicarb (HCO3), magnesium (Mg or mag), and phosphates.

Electrolytes out of balance can indicate volume depletion (dehydration), overhydration, drug reactions or effects, and can be associated with certain diseases such as diabetes insipidus.

Endocrine Panel

Glucose in blood, urine. Ketones. Hemoglobin A1c (glycosylated hemoglobin).

Lab studies to determine the presence or control of diabetes mellitus.

Iron Studies

TIBC (total iron-binding capacity), serum iron, ferritin, transferrin.

Hemoglobin and hematocrit also reflect the proper balance of iron in the system. Excess iron (hemochromatosis) and deficient iron (anemia) can be indicative of major health problems.

Lipid Profile

Triglycerides, cholesterol, LDL (low-density lipids), HDL (high-density lipids).

The values reported in a lipid profile may indicate cardiac risk and predisposition to atherosclerotic heart disease. Abnormal lipid profile values could indicate the likelihood of future artery blockages. The LDL (low-density lipids) and the ratio of HDL to LDL are calculated from the results of the three main components of the panel as listed.

Liver (Hepatic) Function Tests

Albumin, total bilirubin, direct bilirubin, AST, ALT, alkaline phosphatase, LDH (lactic acid dehydrogenase), total protein.

Tests performed to evaluate and monitor liver damage.

Sometimes in complete metabolic panels or liver function testing, SGOT is used instead of AST, standing for serum glutamic-oxaloacetic transaminase, and SGPT is used instead of ALT. It stands for serum glutamic-pyruvic transaminase.

Prostate Specific Antigen/PSA

Test performed to indicate PSA levels to evaluate for possible prostate cancer or the recurrence of it.

A high PSA can indicate the presence of prostatic cancer.

Renal (Or Kidney) Function Tests

BUN (blood urea nitrogen), creatinine, creatinine clearance.

These tests are performed to monitor kidney function and diagnose such conditions as renal insufficiency and chronic kidney disease.

Simultaneous Multichannel Autoanalyzer/SMA

The actual lab equipment that processes samples for analysis.

Sometimes panels of laboratory tests, such as the Chem-7, the basic metabolic panel, or the comprehensive metabolic panel, are referred to as SMA-7, SMA-12, SMA-18, and others, depending on the number of separate chemicals analyzed. All of these are tests for chemicals in the blood. You will notice that several of the items in this list include some of the same studies. The selection of laboratory studies for analysis is dependent, of course, on the medical needs of the patient.

Thyroid Function Tests

T3 uptake, T4, TSH (thyroid-stimulating hormone), thyroxine index.

Thyroid function tests are performed to determine how well the thyroid is working and are used to help diagnose hyperthyroidism (overactive thyroid) and hypothyroidism (underactive thyroid).

Urinalysis

Albumin, pH, specific gravity, RBCs, WBCs, ketones, glucose, protein, nitrites, leukocyte esterase.

Study of the chemistries in the urine can detect the presence of infection, chronic disease, dehydration, overhydration, and a variety of other illnesses and abnormalities.

I. **MULTIPLE CHOICE.**
   Choose the best answer.

1. The test to determine the presence or control of diabetes mellitus is a/an _____.
   - ○ endocrine panel
   - ○ lipid profile
   - ○ SMA
   - ○ urinalysis

2. This test can indicate the presence of prostatic cancer.
   - ○ Hepatic function tests
   - ○ PSA
   - ○ SMA
   - ○ Urinalysis

3. This is the actual lab equipment that processes samples for analysis.
   - ○ SMA
   - ○ PSA
   - ○ Chem-7
   - ○ Lipid profile

4. Chem-7 does not include _____.
   - ○ creatinine
   - ○ electrolytes
   - ○ CO_2
   - ○ serum iron

5. This test can indicate cardiac risk and predisposition to atherosclerotic heart disease.

○ Renal function tests
○ PSA
○ Lipid profile
○ Chem-7

6. Creatinine and creatinine clearance are measured in what type of tests?

○ Liver function tests
○ Arterial blood gas tests
○ Renal function tests
○ Lipid profiles

7. Which of the following do thyroid function tests NOT test for?

○ T3 uptake
○ TSH
○ thyroxine index
○ BUN

8. Iron studies determine levels of _____.

○ BUN, creatinine, creatinine clearance
○ TIBC, ferritin, and transferrin
○ T3 uptake, T4, thyroxine index
○ triglycerides, LDL, HDL

9. Albumin, pH, specific gravity, and protein are tested for in _____.

○ Chem-7
○ LYTES
○ Urinalysis
○ Renal function

10. An electrolytes test is often referred to as _____.

○ electro
○ el
○ trolytes
○ lytes

11. Another name for liver function tests is _____.

○ Thyroid function tests
○ Renal function tests
○ Lipid profile
○ Hepatic function tests

Culture and Sensitivity

Laboratory studies, such as culture and sensitivity (C&S), detect the presence of pathogenic organisms—bacteria, viruses, yeasts, fungi, ova and parasites—as causes of disease so that effective diagnoses and treatments can be assessed and implemented.

These pathogenic organisms are **not** so easy to identify in the transcription editing process, mostly because they can be very challenging to spell. Note, for example, the following bacteria:

- Stenotrophomonas maltophilia
- Escherichia coli
- Staphylococcus aureus
- Yersinia enterocolitica
- Klebsiella pneumoniae
- Actinobacillus actinomycetemcomitans

You should notice immediately that the first element of the organism's name is capped and the second is not. The capped element of the name is the genus; the lower case element of the name is the species. If the only name given is the genus, the term is not capitalized, for example, pseudomonas or clostridium. If the genus is given as short form, such as *strep*, it should not be capitalized either.

These are just a sample. There are hundreds of pathogenic organisms. (Hopefully the dictators pronounce them clearly!)

For those who want to know something more about any of these lab studies or other lab studies that we may not have included here, you can find abundant resource sites on the Internet. Here are some to start with. These sites are good places to find the less commonly seen laboratory tests—the Cortrosyn stim (stimulation) test, immunoglobulins, D-zylose test, or antibody/antigen tests, for example.

www.labtestsonline.org

www.medicinenet.com

Review: Laboratory Studies

I. **MULTIPLE CHOICE.**
   Choose the best answer.

1. A value not included in a CBC.
   ○ hemoglobin
   ○ hematocrit
   ○ sodium
   ○ platelets

2. Iron studies include values for serum iron, ferritin, transferrin, and ___.
   ○ TSH
   ○ TIBC
   ○ LDL
   ○ HDL

3. Test that measures blood components.
   ○ Thyroid function test
   ○ CMP
   ○ Chem-7
   ○ CBC

4. PTT is a part of a ___ study.
   ○ lipid
   ○ coagulation
   ○ glucose
   ○ urinalysis

5. Toxicology screens are performed to detect the presence of ___.
   ○ viruses
   ○ bacteria
   ○ drugs
   ○ anemia

6. The term *hyperthyroidism* means that the thyroid is ___.
   ○ overactive
   ○ underactive
   ○ appropriately active
   ○ absent

7. The terms AST and ALT are respectively interchangeable with ___.
   ○ TSH/SGTP
   ○ GGT/SGPT
   ○ SGOT/SGPT
   ○ TSH/STP

8. The abbreviation *BUN* stands for ___.
   ○ blood urea nephrology
   ○ benzolated urine nephrocytes
   ○ blood urea nitrogen
   ○ best urinalysis number

II. TRUE/FALSE.
Mark the following true or false.

1. A low hemoglobin rules out anemia.
   - ○ true
   - ○ false

2. Abnormal lipid profile values could indicate the likelihood of future artery blockages.
   - ○ true
   - ○ false

3. PSA stands for prostate-separating antigen.
   - ○ true
   - ○ false

4. The doctor dictates, "The patient has strep." The "s" in strep should NOT be capitalized.
   - ○ true
   - ○ false

Laboratory Data in Reports

In the beginning, as a new transcription editor, understanding the laboratory data in a report may seem quite daunting. The dictator is not only using unfamiliar terms and abbreviations, but is throwing in numbers, seemingly at random. In addition, since laboratory reports are often routine, dictators tend to whip through them with amazing speed. The good news is this—because they are routine, time and experience remove the difficulty.

The primary objective of the following lessons is to familiarize you with the order and format of the laboratory data as it appears in medical reports. You will notice that lab reports have a style and punctuation all their own. Complete sentences are not required. The numeric value of the test performed should be recorded either before or after the name of the test (depending on the dictation) separated by only a space. A test such as the CBC may include a variety of subtests, and you should be aware of these and how to punctuate them. As with many things in medical transcription editing, there is acceptable variation to how some of the laboratory information is presented. Keep that in mind as you work through this unit (and the entire training program)—it will help you keep your sanity!

The following lessons are chock full of laboratory snippets from authentic medical reports. Read through the laboratory data sections carefully and pay attention to the format and placement of the numeric values.

Lab Reports – Lesson 1

LABORATORY AND X-RAY FINDINGS: Her laboratory studies showed a sodium of 143, potassium of 3.8, chloride of 97, bicarbonate of 30, BUN of 9, and white count of 11,900. X-rays showed a small effusion at the left base. Abdominal films showed a normal amount of gas with no air-fluid levels.

LABORATORY DATA: White count 36.8, H&H 10.9 and 33.7. Urine showed a specific gravity of 1.031.[1] Chest x-ray showed a right upper lobe infiltrate.

LABORATORY FINDINGS: A white count was 23.7 with 41 segs and 1 band. Hemoglobin of 8.6, hematocrit of 27.3. A cath UA[2] showed 1+ blood, 30-35 white cells, and 1+ rods.

LABORATORY DATA: Initial laboratory work showed a sodium of 147, potassium 3.6, chloride 102, bicarb 32.1, glucose 136. Liver function tests were completely within normal limits. CBC showed white count of 5700,[3] H&H 11.4 and 33.6, with 287,000 platelets.

LABORATORY DATA: On admission, white blood cell count 12.8 with 5 segs, 6 bands, 83 lymphs, 5 monos, and 1 baso. Hemoglobin was 9.4, hematocrit 27.1 with platelet count of 347. VBG[4] showed pH of 7.4 and pCO2 of 34. Urinalysis was negative. Cerebrospinal fluid labs showed a protein of 61, glucose 46, no red blood cells, 4 white blood cells (1 poly, 3 lymphs). On Gram stain, there were no organisms seen. Lytes[5] were within normal limits.

Footnotes:

1. This specific gravity would be dictated as "ten thirty-one," but is edited correctly as 1.031.

2. A *cath* UA is one collected via catheter.

3. A number with four numerals can be edited with or without a comma, both 5700 and 5,700 are acceptable.

4. VBG is venous blood gas, as opposed to arterial blood gas.

5. Lytes is short for electrolytes.

I. **SPELLING.**
   Determine if the following words are spelled correctly. If the spelling is correct, leave the word as it has already been entered. If the spelling is incorrect, provide the correct spelling.

   1. sodium _____

   2. bicarbonnate _____

   3. protien _____

   4. hemoglobin _____

   5. hemotocrit _____

   6. potasium _____

   7. specific gravity _____

   8. uranalysis _____

   9. BUN _____

   10. platlets _____

Lab Reports – Lesson 2

Medical Record

LABORATORY DATA: Hemoglobin 5.6, hematocrit 18, MCV 68 with MCHC of 31 and MCH 21. Liver enzymes and clotting times were normal.

LABORATORY DATA: White count 14.2 with 45 segs, 32 bands, 20 lymphs, and 3 monos. Hemoglobin was 11.2, hematocrit 34, and platelet count 286. UA was negative. Sodium was 141, potassium 4.3, chloride 98, bicarb 25, glucose 101, BUN 12, creatinine 0.3. Uric acid 3.9, phosphate 5.1, calcium 9.6, and magnesium 2.3.

LABORATORY DATA: Sodium 139, potassium 3.7, chloride 107, total CO2 of 25, creatinine 1.6, glucose 131, CPK of 257, phosphorus 2.9, alkaline phosphatase of 123, total protein 6.7, LDH 151, albumin 3.7, SGOT 23, PTT 40, PT 11.7, magnesium 2.0, total bilirubin 0.6. White cell count 7.5, hematocrit 42.1 with an MCV of 88.4, platelet count 154.

LABORATORY DATA: The urinalysis was negative. White blood cell count was 2.6, hemoglobin 11.7, MCV 93.2, platelet count 150,000. CD4 count was 35. Serum electrolytes: sodium 144, potassium 4.1, chloride 114, CO2 of 23,[1] glucose 82, creatinine 1.4, calcium 9.2, albumin 3.7, bilirubin 0.5, SGOT 62, LDH 234, SGPT 40.

LABORATORY DATA ON ADMISSION: Remarkable for a creatinine of 1.4 and a potassium of 3.5. A urinalysis shows a specific gravity of 1.015, pH 6.5, 100 protein, moderate blood, 4 white blood cells per high-powered field, and 9 red blood cells per high-powered field. Discharge labs are significant for a creatinine of 2.2 and a hematocrit of 31.6.

Footnotes:

1. Even if dictated simply as CO2 23, it is generally preferred to put "of" between the consecutive numbers 2 and 2.

I. MULTIPLE CHOICE.
Choose the correct term for the abbreviation expansion.

1. MCV – mean (◯corpuscular, ◯cortical) volume

2. CO2 – carbon (◯dioxide, ◯dating)

3. BUN – blood (◯urine, ◯urea) nitrogen

4. PT – (◯prothrombin, ◯partial) time

5. PTT – partial (◯thromboplastin, ◯thrombolitic) time

Medical Record

LABORATORY AND X-RAY FINDINGS: She had initially a white blood cell count of 15.7, H&H of 11.9 and 35.6. BUN and creatinine were within normal limits. Her urinalysis showed 3+ bacteria, 2+ occult blood. Urine culture grew out E. coli greater than 100,000 organisms. Followup labs showed white blood cell count climbing to 29,000, and after treatment lowered to 19,000. A followup urine culture did not grow out any E. coli after antibiotic treatment.

LABORATORY AND X-RAY FINDINGS: Chest x-ray on admission showed a large consolidation of the right upper lobe with a questionable infiltrate versus atelectasis in the right middle lobe. His white count was 16.5 with 44 segs, 44 bands, and 10 lymphocytes. His hemoglobin was 13.4, hematocrit 39.9, platelet count 227. Urine showed a specific gravity of 1.012 with 1+ blood, 1+ protein. Electrolytes were remarkable for a slightly low potassium of 3.2. His liver function studies and amylase were normal. ABGs showed pH of 7.4, pCO_2 and pO_2 within normal ranges.

LABORATORY AND X-RAY FINDINGS: Chest x-ray shows a left upper lobe pneumonia. Blood cultures were drawn. Glucose 125, sodium 144, potassium 5.3, chloride 97, CO_2 29, BUN 11, creatinine 0.2. White blood cell count was 58.9, hemoglobin 10.2, hematocrit 33.0, differential showing 55 segs, 16 bands, 23 lymphs, and 3 monos. UA: specific gravity 1.024, 0-1 white blood cells, and 0-1 RBCs. Spinal fluid showed 2 polys, 4 RBCs. Gram stain: 3+ protein.

LABORATORY DATA: Chem-7 unremarkable. White blood count 8.7, hemoglobin 13.1, hematocrit 39.4, platelets 728,000, MCV 113, macrocytosis 2+. Calcium, magnesium, phosphorus essentially normal. LFTs normal. CSF studies showed glucose and protein within normal limits.

I. MATCHING.
Match the correct term to the definition.

1. ____ Hidden, obscure, not obvious on observation.

2. ____ Sugar.

3. ____ Sodium, potassium, chloride, bicarbonate.

4. ____ Incomplete expansion of a lung or portion of a lung.

5. ____ A chemical in the blood or urine that is used in the diagnostic analysis of kidney function.

6. ____ A condition characterized by larger than normal erythrocytes.

7. ____ Disk-shaped structures found in blood that help coagulate blood.

8. ____ Segmented neutrophils, lymphocytes, monocytes.

A. atelectasis
B. macrocytosis
C. occult
D. platelets
E. creatinine
F. glucose
G. electrolyte
H. white blood cells

Normal Laboratory Values

As a medical transcription editor, you must have at least a general understanding of normal laboratory values. There may be times when an author dictates a value mistakenly, and, as an efficient medical transcription editor, it is up to you to catch these types of errors and bring them to the attention of QA or the client, depending on the procedure followed by your employer. Lab value errors can adversely affect patient care, so it is of the utmost importance that the values be reported correctly. In this lesson, we will look at normal values for some of the more common tests. This list is not meant to be comprehensive by any means, but it will cover values that will frequently pop up during your career as an MTE. We have also included some notes that may be helpful along the way. Normal ranges that differ from male to female are notated with M and F.

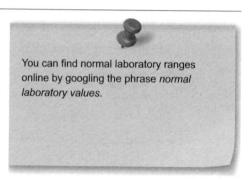

You can find normal laboratory ranges online by googling the phrase *normal laboratory values*.

Frequently Dictated CBC Components

Lab Test	Normal Range	Information
White Blood Cell Count (WBC)	3800–11,000 (may be expressed as 3.8–11.0 thousand)	High levels usually indicate bacterial infection.
Neutrophils	50%–81%	High levels may indicate active infection.
Lymphocytes	14%–44%	Elevated level may indicate viral infection.
Monocytes	2%–6%	Elevated level may indicate chronic infection or cancer.

Eosinophils	1%–5%	Elevated level may indicate allergic reaction or parasites.
Basophils	0%–1%	Elevated level may indicate allergic reaction or chronic inflammation.
Red blood cells (rbc's)	M 4.2–5.6, F 3.8–5.1	If rbc's are low, then hemoglobin and hematocrit (H&H) will most likely also be low.
Hemoglobin	M 14–18 g/dL, F 12–16 g/dL	Amount of O2 carrying protein in blood, gives blood red color. Low level indicates anemia.
Hematocrit	M 39%–54%, F 34%–47%	Percentage of blood that is occupied by red blood cells. Low level may indicate anemia.
Platelets	140,000–450,000 /ml	Platelets play an important role in blood clotting.

Frequently Dictated CMP Components

Lab Test	Normal Range	Information
Sodium	135–148 mEq/L	Low levels (hyponatremia) may lead to seizures or other neurological problems.
Potassium	3.5–5.5 mEq/L	Elevation (hyperkalemia) can indicate renal failure or diabetes; low levels (hypokalemia) can lead to heart arrhythmia.
Chloride	96–112 mEq/L	Abnormal levels may indicate kidney problems.
CO2 (or bicarbonate)	22–30 mmol/L	Helps to maintain acidity level in bodily fluids.
BUN	6–23 mg/dL	Elevated levels may indicate such events as heart failure, excessive protein intake, or that the kidneys are just not functioning properly.
Creatinine	0.6–1.5 mg/dL	Low or high levels could indicate kidney damage.
Glucose	65–99 mg/dL	Sustained elevation above normal range may indicate diabetes. Below normal range is hypoglycemia, and above normal range is hyperglycemia.
Calcium	8–11 mg/dL	Calcium is important for such processes as proper cardiac function, bone metabolism, and protein absorption.

Frequently Dictated Lipoproteins and Triglycerides

Lab Test	Normal Range
Cholesterol, total	< 200 mg/dL
HDL cholesterol	30–70 mg/dL
LDL cholesterol	65–180 mg/dL
Triglycerides	45–155 mg/dL (< 160)
AST (SGOT)	< 35 IU/L (ideal 20-48)
ALT (SGPT)	< 35 IU/L

Review: Normal Laboratory Values

I. MULTIPLE CHOICE.
Choose the best answer.

1. The physician dictates what sounds like the following: "WBC 9000, hemoglobin 46, hematocrit 39, platelets 263,000." Which value is likely incorrect (misstated or misunderstood)?
   - ○ WBC
   - ○ hemoglobin
   - ○ hematocrit
   - ○ platelets

2. The following is dictated for CMP results, but the blanked word cannot be understood in the dictation: "Sodium 139, potassium 4.2, chloride 99, CO2 29, BUN 15, ___ 0.9, glucose 98, calcium 9." Ruling out all other possibilities and listening to the dictation again, what would the most likely missing component be?
   - ○ hemoglobin
   - ○ iron
   - ○ creatinine
   - ○ alkaline phosphatase

3. Which of the following values would be considered normal?
   - ○ hemoglobin 13
   - ○ BUN 40
   - ○ glucose 240
   - ○ creatinine 2.9

4. The physician dictates, "WBC 8300, H&H 13.7 and 37.2, respectively." The hematocrit value is ___.
   - ○ 13.7
   - ○ 37.2
   - ○ 8300
   - ○ None of the above

5. A patient with a glucose of 266 would be considered ___.
   - ○ anemic
   - ○ cachectic
   - ○ hypoglycemic
   - ○ hyperglycemic

II. TRUE/FALSE.
Mark the following true or false.

1. A patient with a WBC of 3800 almost certainly has a bacterial infection.
   - ○ true
   - ○ false

2. Hyperkalemia means an elevated potassium level.
   - ○ true
   - ○ false

3. Hyponatremia may lead to seizures.
   - ○ true
   - ○ false

4. A total cholesterol level of 225 is considered to be within normal range.
   - ○ true
   - ○ false

5. An elevated creatinine could indicate kidney problems.
   - ○ true
   - ○ false

Laboratory Data Helpful Tips

The new MTE may find laboratory data particularly daunting; but be assured that it gets easier with experience. Transcription editing of laboratory data will eventually become almost second nature. There are a few important tips to remember to help you edit laboratory data with accuracy and efficiency.

- **Never guess** at a laboratory value. Keep in mind that patients are receiving treatment based on these values, and incorrect values could adversely affect patient care, possibly leading to incorrect medication doses and even death of a patient.
- Question dictated values if they are far out of line with normal or abnormal ranges. For example, if you think the physician is dictating a creatinine of 380, be sure to question it by following the appropriate process recommended by your employer. Remember, physicians are human and they can make mistakes, too. It is always safer to question a value rather than to just edit incorrect information.
- You may find it helpful to keep a comprehensive printout of normal laboratory values handy, because dictated laboratory components vary from client to client, physician to physician.

Unit 9
Formatting

Formatting – Introduction

Rules, standards, and *preferences*: These are but a few of the words you will encounter when your future employer, company, or client utilizes your services as a transcription editor. The rules, standards, and preferences of how the document is prepared are all a part of the formatting process we will be covering in this unit.

Merriam-Webster defines format as "a method of organizing data… the general plan of arrangement or choice of material." Quite simply, formatting is a facet of medical transcription editing that further enhances the integrity, quality, and consistency of the document with that of the proposed standard/style.

Imagine you are taking your dog for a walk and a passer-by in an SUV flags you down to ask for directions to an area theater. He has a pen and paper handy, so you take the time to explain how to get there and draw an outline reflecting his path of travel. You might use octagons for stop signs, arrows to indicate turns, and squares to indicate buildings. Another person might use circles for stop signs, dotted lines to indicate a path, and forego the use of landmarks in order to get the lost driver to his destination. The way the map is drawn and the details that went into its creation are, rough though they might be, formatting styles.

Similarly, in medical transcription editing, Account A might insist that all reports be edited verbatim, meaning word for word. Account B, however, might require reports to be edited with a specific set of guidelines in place. Spelling and grammatical errors, idiomatic phrases and expressions, as well as slang phrases and lab data language are all areas that might be affected by account-specific instructions, or formatting preferences.

Medicine, like all aspects of life, evolves and changes. It is impossible to create a unit in which all-inclusive instructions are given in terms of medical document formatting. What we can do, however, is provide an overview of the types of styles, rules, and formatting specifics you might encounter when editing. Your future employer will provide you with specifics in order to apply these styles and preferences to the documents you edit.

Formatting and Industry Trends

The format of a medical report will vary according to the individual client. Your future employer will provide you with account specifications (also known as account instructions). Part of your job is to ensure these rules and specifications are carried out and adhered to properly. Although all rules are subject to change from specific clients, there are general industry guidelines that apply to all of medical transcription editing (unless specifically contraindicated by the client). These include things such as medications, dates, abbreviations, usage and placement of numbers, and so forth. An overview of these style issues will be provided in this unit.

There are medical transcription editing industry standards, practices, and trends that, fortunately for you, will never change and are quite static in their very nature. For example, it is generally unacceptable to begin a sentence with a number, as illustrated below.

Dictated: 12 days ago, the patient began to feel sluggish, diaphoretic, and lightheaded.

Edited: Twelve days ago, the patient began to feel sluggish, diaphoretic, and lightheaded.

Remember those exceptions you read about? Some clients might allow a sentence to begin with a year: "2007 was the doctor's busiest year so far." However, some might prefer and allow the transcription editor to recast the sentence: "The doctor's busiest year so far was 2007." Within this context, you will be instructed as to whether *flagging* (using a pend note) is necessary in such situations. *Flagging* is an account-specified way to highlight or draw attention to a potential error, missing data, indistinguishable information, or even inconsistent information. Again, the company that employs you will have a specific protocol in place for handling such situations and how they will expect you to adhere to the protocol.

All of this may seem a bit overwhelming at this point. You might be thinking, how am I supposed to remember all of these terms, forms, standards, procedures, rules, and now exceptions to those rules? If you can read, write, and speak English (and we know you can) then you've already mastered one of the most difficult languages to learn in the world. The beauty of that is you will be applying your knowledge of English, verbs agreement, tenses, commas, etc. to medical transcription editing. Medicine evolves and there are aspects of it that are ever-changing. English language rules are, for the most part, set in stone. However, client A might want their formatting done according to one set of rules while client B might want a slight variation on those rules. Having those documents handy to refer to as you learn account instructions will help you tremendously. For now, having an overview of what to expect and what those rules, standards, and specifications might look like is a good starting point.

General Formatting Rules

In general, there are some industry rules or trends that rarely change according to account or client. Bear in mind there are always exceptions, but for the most part these are general rules you will be expected to adhere to as a medical transcription editor. (Consider these sort of the default styles for the industry.)

Abbreviations

Do not use abbreviations in any diagnosis lists (admission, discharge, pre/postoperative), impressions, or lists/names of procedures and operations. For example, if in the list of diagnoses a doctor states, "TIA," and you can be 100% certain that this means transient ischemic attack by the content/ context of the report, you would instead edit to "transient ischemic attack" in place of TIA.

Never abbreviate a word that a doctor dictates in full. Although it may be tempting to shorten a word into an abbreviation to save keystrokes and get done quicker, do not do so. For example, if a doctor states "myocardial infarction," do **not** edit to MI.

Abbreviations **are** to be used for metric units of measure used in medical reports when a numeric quantity precedes the unit of measure. For example, "A 2-cm lesion was located" or "Her blood pressure was 120/80 mmHg." Never add an "s" to pluralize a metric unit of measure.

Slang

Edit in full any slang terms. Doctors use slang terms often in medical reports. Examples are: alk phos is 78 (instead of alkaline phosphatase), an appy in 1984 (instead of appendectomy), and scope was withdrawn (instead of laryngoscope or some other kind of scope). **Unless otherwise instructed**, you are to edit to the full and appropriate word or words. (It should be noted that we say "unless otherwise instructed" because verbatim transcription editing is becoming more and more common in the industry—which means more and more slang is being edited as dictated.)

Flags

Some words are to be flagged, omitted, or left blank. Obscenities, derogatory remarks, and double entendres (words that have varied meanings, one of which could be perceived as inappropriate or insensitive) are all examples of types of language that should be avoided. In general, obscene words are not to be used unless instructed by the client (or in many cases, part of a direct quotation).

Brief Forms

Use brief forms only when dictated. A brief form is a word that has been shortened and is acceptable as a shortened version. Some of the most common of these are exam, prepped, Pap smear, temp, and sed rate. These are acceptable only if they are dictated as such. (You may be thinking what makes one word slang and another a brief form.) Unfortunately and fortunately, if things like slang versus brief forms are not outlined specifically by your account instructions, there will be acceptable variation to how you present this type of information.

mmHg

The abbreviation for millimeters of mercury is mmHg. This is a common term used with pressure readings, such as blood pressure and tourniquet pressure. If you do abbreviate it, you should use the correct form, which is mmHg. A period is not to be used unless mmHg falls at the end of a sentence.

> Dictated: The patient's blood pressure was 113 over 84 millimeters of mercury.
>
> Edited: The patient's blood pressure was 113/84 mmHg.
>
> Dictated: Her pressure was 139 over 69 millimeters of mercury earlier and it has since normalized.
>
> Edited: Her pressure was 139/69 mmHg earlier and it has since normalized.

pH

NEVER capitalize the p in pH. The term pH is used to designate alkalinity and it should **NEVER** be capitalized. If it is dictated first in a sentence, add the word "the" or recast the sentence, according to client/account instructions.

> Dictated: ph was 7.3.
>
> Edited: The pH was 7.3.

Dates

Dates are to be written out unless otherwise specified. Your client will probably have a preference for the way dates are designated; for example, in the military they are entered as day/month/year in the following manner: 10 Feb 93. It can also be appropriate to edit as 2-10-93 or 2/10/93, if so requested. But, if there is no specific requirement, dates should be spelled out in the body of a report, as in February 10, 1993. The good news—the patient information has been washed from the practicum reports in this training program in order to protect patient confidentiality. This means you will not be editing dates in our practicum. It is important for you to understand, however, that there are a number of ways to correctly present dates.

Allergies

If a patient has allergies, a special font or format is usually used in order to draw attention to them. Some accounts/clients prefer all caps for allergies, as in: ALLERGIES: ERYTHROMYCIN AND ASPIRIN. Others may use italics, special formatting, or any form of character encoding so that allergies are clearly distinguished and alerted from the rest of the report contents.

Numbers

When editing numbers the issues are whether to use Arabic versus Roman and whether to spell out the number (for example, seven) or use the numeral (7) instead. Within this unit, specifics as to the preferred usage of numbers will be examined. In general, most numbers that you will edit will be Arabic unless Roman is the usage mandated, and most numbers will be presented as the numerals instead of being spelled out (again, this is just in general).

I. **TRUE/FALSE.**
   Mark the following true or false.

1. All edited medical reports follow the same set of standards for formatting.

   ○ true
   ○ false

2. In medical transcription editing, it is generally not accepted to begin a sentence with a number.

   ○ true
   ○ false

3. Flagging is a way of passing a report on to another transcription editor to finish.

   ○ true
   ○ false

4. Slang terms should always be edited exactly as they are dictated.

   ○ true
   ○ false

5. The abbreviation mmHg is the appropriate abbreviation for millimeters of mercury.

   ○ true
   ○ false

Book of Style

One of the references you will encounter in the industry is called the *Book of Style for Medical Transcription*, which is a stylistic and practical book of guidelines and preferences dealing with medical transcription editing, its informational points of grammar, punctuation, and usage. The Book of Style is a product of the Association for Healthcare Documentation Integrity (AHDI), formerly known as American Association for Medical Transcription (AAMT). As stated earlier, there are many styles and variations in formatting that will be presented to you in your training and eventual employment as a medical transcription editor, and the Book of Style is one of them. The Book of Style is included in the KB Benchmark tool. We will refer to some of the standards within that context in this section of the formatting unit. (Of note, the information in this unit is based on the *BOS 3E*, the *Book of Style for Medical Transcription, 3rd Edition*.)

You may want to refer back to this unit after you have had an opportunity to practice and work through the medical transcription editing content. For now, take the time to review these standards and be aware that there are acceptable variations and your future employer(s) and accounts will provide instruction and specifics detailing their preferences.

The pages contained in this lesson will outline an array of Book of Style standards. The exercises incorporated into the lesson will test your knowledge of the material presented. All quoted material indicates AHDI BOS 3E as the reference source.

Acronyms

Acronyms are abbreviations formed from the initial letters of each of the successive words (or major parts of a compound term or selected letter of a word or phrase) that is pronounced as a single word.

Some examples of medical and non-medical acronyms:

- AIDS – acquired immune deficiency syndrome
- GERD – gastroesophageal reflux disease
- CABG – coronary artery bypass graft
- LIMA – left internal mammary artery
- OSHA – Occupational Safety and Health Administration
- SADD – Students Against Drunk Driving

Some acronyms derived from initial letters are NOT capitalized. Examples of some are:

- scuba – self-contained underwater breathing apparatus
- laser – light amplification by stimulated emission of radiation
- radar – radio detection and ranging

Acronyms are to be edited as dictated unless otherwise indicated or instructed.

Initialisms

An **initialism** is similar to an acronym in that it is "formed from the initial letter of each of the successive words (or major parts of a compound term or of selected letters of a word or phrase) that is **not** pronounced as a word, but by each letter." This is easy to remember because an initialism is just that, a grouping of initials that you would **not** say aloud as you would an acronym.

Some examples of medical and non-medical initialisms:

- CPR – cardiopulmonary resuscitation
- VCR – videocassette recorder
- R&D – research and development
- LMP – last menstrual period
- GFM – good fetal movement
- CBBB – complete bundle branch block
- BGRS – blood glucose reagent strip

Abbreviations and Brief Forms

Abbreviations

An **abbreviation** is a shortened form of a word or a phrase that is used in place of the whole. Abbreviations are prevalent in the world of medicine. According to BOS 3, it is generally preferred to write out an abbreviation or acronym in full if it is used in the admission, discharge, preoperative, or postoperative diagnosis; in the consultative conclusion; or in the operative title. Non-disease-entity abbreviations accompanying diagnostic and procedure statements may be used if dictated. (It is preferable to abbreviate units of measure.) When you are unable to translate an abbreviation or shortened form within one of these sections, you would normally flag it for attention.

Dangerous Abbreviations

The Institute for Safe Medication Practices (ISMP) has designated a list of abbreviations that are deemed dangerous to the patient's safety according to how they are edited. This list appears in your BOS 3E pages 206–213. You can also find a PDF copy of the ISMP Dangerous Abbreviations list by visiting the following link: http://www.ismp.org/tools/errorproneabbreviations.pdf.

Examples of abbreviations:

- WBC (white blood count)
- USMC (United States Marine Corps)
- t.v. (television)
- TB (tuberculosis)

State and territory names should be abbreviated if they are preceded by a city, a state, or a territory name. States should be abbreviated in an address. Names of states, territories, and countries should not be abbreviated if they are used alone. The following illustrate some examples of this rule:

My brother was taken to an operating room in Kansas City, MO, when we visited recently.

I am looking forward to seeing the specialist in California.

Drug Terminology Abbreviations and Punctuation

Drug dosages are often abbreviated and kept "as is," when editing. The following list should **not** be translated/expanded.

Abbreviation	English Translation
a.c.	before food
b.i.d.	twice a day
gtt.	drops (preferred if you spell out drops)
n.p.o.	nothing by mouth
n.r.	do not repeat
p.c.	after food

p.o.	by mouth
p.r.n.	as needed
q.4 h.	every 4 hours (note the space: q.4 h. is used for clarity)
q.h.	every hour
q.i.d.	4 times a day
t.i.d.	3 times a day
u.d.	as directed

Brief Forms

Brief forms are commonplace in medical transcription editing. Some are acceptable and some are not. Brief forms are simply shortened forms of words. Brief forms are to be edited as dictated unless they appear in headings, diagnoses, and operative titles. You should lowercase the brief form unless it is routinely capitalized. An ending period is not used, and the plural of a brief form is accomplished by adding the letter *s* without an apostrophe. On the job, some of your accounts may prefer expansion of brief forms, and some brief forms are not acceptable at all.

Examples of some brief forms both medical and non-medical:

- phone
- Pap smear
- exam
- segs
- cath
- infarct
- fax
- temp

I. **MULTIPLE CHOICE.**
   Choose the best answer.

   1. An example of an acronym is ___.
      ○ WBC
      ○ p.r.n.
      ○ CPR
      ○ CABG

   2. The abbreviation p.o. translates to ___.
      ○ by mouth
      ○ as needed
      ○ every morning
      ○ before food

3. An initialism is ___.

   ⭕ A shortened form of a word or a phrase which is used in place of the whole.

   ⭕ A grouping of initials that you would NOT say aloud as you would an acronym.

   ⭕ Formed from the initial letters of words or major parts of a compound term.

   ⭕ Sometimes known as brief forms.

4. The word *temp* in medical terminology is an example of a/an ___.

   ⭕ abbreviation

   ⭕ brief form

   ⭕ initialism

   ⭕ acronym

5. Twice a day would be edited as ___.

   ⭕ b.i.d.

   ⭕ t.i.d.

   ⭕ t.a.d.

   ⭕ n.p.o.

II. **MATCHING.**
   Match the abbreviation with the appropriate translation.

   1. ___ do not repeat

   2. ___ as directed

   3. ___ after food

   4. ___ every hour

   5. ___ drops

   A. q.h.
   B. u.d.
   C. n.r.
   D. gtt.
   E. p.c.

Eponyms

What the dictator may say: After parturition, the patient complained of alopecia, cephalgia, and pain over the cicatrix. The on-call attending ordered lab tests of FSH in addition to testing the hypophysis.

What the dictator means: After childbirth, the patient complained of hair loss, headache, and pain over the scar. The on-call attending ordered lab tests of FSH, follicle-stimulating hormone, in addition to testing the pituitary gland.

Question: Why don't dictators just speak in plain English?

Answer: Because this isn't plain English—it's the medical language. As medical transcription editors, we have to know what the doctor means. Patient document integrity, risk management, and quality assurance all depend on it.

An **eponym** is a name, such as drug, disease, operation, or anatomic structure, based on or derived from a person or a place. Examples of some medical eponyms are:

- Alzheimer disease
- Down syndrome
- Parkinson disease
- Cushing syndrome
- Addison disease
- Pap (Papanicolaou) smear

If the eponym takes a possessive form, then the BOS 3E prefers and recommends dropping the apostrophe s ('s) as in:

- Apgar score
- Hodgkin lymphoma
- Gram stain
- Arnold-Chiari malformation
- Guillain-Barre syndrome
- Crohn disease
- Klatskin tumor

Exceptions to the Eponym Rule

HOWEVER—and that is capitalized because this is really important—not every apostrophe s ('s) is dropped in eponyms. While the possessive form remains an acceptable alternative, BOS indicates the use of an apostrophe s as preferred by client or employer. Further, some eponyms end in the letter s, and in those cases, the s is to be kept in place. Examples are:

- Homans sign
- Christmas factor
- Bundle of His
- Pouch of Douglas
- Pores of Kohn
- Brill-Symmers disease
- Libman-Sacks disease
- Riggs disease
- Williams syndrome

Unfortunately, there is no magic wand to wave and commit these instantaneously to memory. Your on-the-job experience and hands-on dictation practicum will benefit you greatly in successfully embracing the sometimes possessive nature of medicine.

Slang

Dictators frequently use slang, jargon, or shortened forms, and we hardly even recognize them as such because they have become so commonplace. While abbreviated forms are often acceptable, the same thing is not necessarily true of slang. In formal medical documents it is better to avoid slang terms and phrases unless the meaning cannot be determined otherwise (which is a very rare occurrence) or when they more accurately communicate the meaning (also a rare occurrence).

Account instructions will vary from account to account, but AHDI's stance on slang and phrases is to avoid them except when essential to the report and/or when the actual slang/phrase more accurately communicates meaning than translating them would. Also, if the meaning cannot be determined, it is recommended to leave as-is.

You have already covered slang terms in the Mastering the Medical Language module, but here is a review of some commonly heard slang terms in medical reports. Of course, there are manuals, reference guides, and even slang dictionaries dedicated solely to this topic. Hence, the list below is but a smattering of some of the "slanguage" dictators utter in the course of their reporting day.

Slang	Expanded Form
a-fib, A-fi, AFib	atrial fibrillation
alk phos	alkaline phosphatase
appy	appendectomy or appendicitis
bicarb	bicarbonate
bili	bilirubin
CBC with diff	CBC (complete blood count) with differential
caps	capsules
cath	catheter or catheterization
chemo	chemotherapy
chole	cholecystectomy
crit	hematocrit
DC	discontinue or discharge
detox	detoxification
dig	digoxin or digitalis
dip sesta	dipyridamole sestamibi
double J stent	JJ stent
echo	echocardiogram
eos	eosinophils
flex sig	flexible sigmoidoscopy
Foley	Foley catheter
HCTZ	hydrochlorothiazide
hem/onc	hematology/oncology
hep C (A, B)	hepatitis C (A, B)
K	potassium
KCl	potassium chloride
lac	laceration
lymphs	lymphocytes
lytes	electrolytes
mag	magnesium

meds	medications
mg	milligrams
mcg	micrograms
monos	monocytes
nebs	nebulizers
neuro	neurological or neurology
neuropsych	neuropsychiatry
O2 sat	oxygen saturation
path	pathology
perf	perforation
preop	preoperative
postop	postoperative
prepped	prepared
psych	psychiatry or psychology
pulse ox	pulse oximetry
regurg	regurgitation
rehab	rehabilitation
sat	saturation
sed rate	sedimentation rate
segs	segmented neutrophils
t. bili	total bilirubin
tabs	tablets
triple A, AAA	abdominal aortic aneurysm
V-tach	ventricular tachycardia
voc rehab	vocational rehabilitation

I. **MULTIPLE CHOICE.**
   Choose the best answer.

1. The correct expanded form for mcg is (◯micrograms, ◯milligrams).

2. Slang for perforation is often called (◯perfo, ◯perf).

3. (◯Alzheimer, ◯Alzheimer's) disease affects a person's memory and cognition.

4. KCl is an abbreviation for (◯potassium nitrate, ◯potassium chloride).

5. CBC with diff means CBC with (◯difference, ◯differential).

6. The (◯bundle of Hi's, ◯bundle of His) deals with the conduction system of the heart.

7. An appendectomy or appendicitis is sometimes called (◯appy, ◯append) in slang.

8. Dip sesta is slang for (◯dypyridamole sestamibi, ◯dipyridamole sestamibi).

9. Pap smear is an example of a/an (◯eponym, ◯synonym).

10. Saturation is sometimes called (◯sat, ◯sit) in slang.

Foreign Terms

A word is a word is a word—unless it's Latin, then it's a translated word. The medical field is full of foreign terms that mingle among common English terms. Unfortunately, the spelling patterns for foreign terms differ from language to language, and doctors may use French, Latin, and Greek terms all in the same report. Luckily, many of these terms become commonplace and you will become well acquainted with them through using them. Note that some terms in the list include periods. AHDI's stance is that periods are the preferred style.

Latin	English	Abbreviation
exempli grata	for example	e.g. or eg
et alii	and others	et al. or et al
et cetera	and so forth	etc. or etc
id est	that is	i.e. or ie
videlicet	that is, namely	viz. or viz

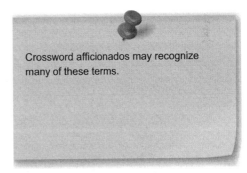

Crossword afficionados may recognize many of these terms.

Foreign Term	English Equivalent
peau d'orange	dimpling of the skin, as seen in breast cancer
grand mal	severe epilepsy characterized by tonic-clonic seizures
mittelschmerz	abdominal pain occurring between menstrual periods
steinstrasse	lithotripsy
lavage	the act of washing
cafe au lait spot	skin lesion that is coffee colored
en bloc	in one block
in toto	as a whole
en masse	in mass
raphe	seam
oculus uterque	each eye

ersatz	synthetic or artificial
en face	head on
mal de mer	seasickness
cerclage	encircling with a loop or ring, as in an incompetent cervix
ad libitum	according to your pleasure
statim	at once
status quo	the existing condition
coup	a hit or stroke
sitz (bath)	type of bath in which only the hips and buttocks are soaked in water or saline solution

The most important thing for you, the MTE, is knowing what these terms mean in the context in which they are used.

I. **SPELLING.**
   Determine if the following words are spelled correctly. If the spelling is correct, leave the word as it has already been entered. If the spelling is incorrect, retype the word with the correct spelling.

1. mittelschmerz _____

2. peau d'orange _____

3. circlage _____

4. sitze _____

5. en mass _____

6. coup _____

7. steinstrasie _____

8. raphie _____

9. add libitum _____

10. levage _____

11. cafe au lait spot _____

12. grand mall _____

13. statim _____

14. en bloc _____

15. staus quoe _____

Numbers

The trend in medical transcription editing is to steer away from the use of Roman numerals and to use Arabic numbers instead (unless your company, client, or account specifies their usage). Arabic numerals are 0 through 9.

Some things to keep in mind when editing numbers according to BOS:

- **Arabic numbers are to be used, as opposed to editing the numbers spelled out.**

  For example, *The patient was rushed to the emergency room within 30 minutes of the accident.*

  Exception: When there are 2 numbers which are consecutive in a sentence, spell one of them out to avoid confusion as in: *The surgeon inserted three 4-inch drains into the wound site.*

- **When editing units of measurement, use the Arabic numeral and abbreviate the measurement.**

  For example, it should be *5 mg, 10 mm, 150 mg*, etc. NOT *ten mm* or *5 millimeters.*

- **Express a ratio with the number and a colon.**

  For example, *head circumference to abdominal circumference ratio is 1:2.*

- **Express a range with the word "to" or a hyphen.**

  For example, *his blood sugars ranged from 78-123* OR *78 to 123.*

- **Use a hyphen to express suture size.**

  This may also be designated by the correct number of zeros, but is more difficult to read: *0000000000 suture for eye surgery.*

  A suture is defined by a certain number of zeros (designating the thickness of the suture material: the larger the number, the smaller the diameter of the suture material). For example, *We used 3-0 Vicryl to close the skin.*

- **Use Arabic digits to number vertebrae and intervertebral spaces.**

  For example, *She had an L4-5 spondylolisthesis. She had a T3 compression fracture.*

  Of note, some clients will delineate vertebrae with hyphens, others with commas: *L4-5; L4,5; T10-11; T10,11.* The hyphenated form is generally preferred, however. It is preferable to repeat the vertebral letter before each vertebra listed, as in: *The herniation involves C5, C6, and C7.*

- **When using a slash in place of the word per, also abbreviate the units of measurement.**

  For example, do not type *15 milligrams/second*, but *15 mg/sec.*

- **Use Arabic digits with symbols, abbreviations, and laboratory values.**

  For example, *CO2 38, pH 7.3, LDH 7, alkaline phosphatase 73.*

- **Use digits with units of measurement.**

  For example, *The specimen was 4 cm x 6 cm x 2 cm.*

- **Use a zero digit and a decimal to designate values of less than one, but do not ADD a decimal and zero for values of one or greater.**

  For example, *0.25% lidocaine was used*, but not *120.0 cc of fluid was given.*

- **Edit a blood pressure reading with numbers and a slash.**

  For example, *Blood pressure was 113/73.*

- **Use Arabic digits to designate Apgar scores.**

For example, *Apgars were 8 and 9.* (This is the visual test performed on a newborn infant at one and five minutes.)

- **Roman numerals are used to express stages with a few exceptions.**

Periods are not to be used with Roman numerals, and they are to be capitalized unless otherwise directed. Examples of usage and exceptions:

A stage II decubitus ulcer

A stage 2 femoral neck Garden fracture

Cancer of the left ovary, FIGO stage III

- **Cranial nerves may be Arabic or Roman.**

Cranial nerve notation is according to client specifications, as in *cranial nerves 2-12* or *cranial nerves II-XII.*

- **Ordinal numbers indicate position or order in a series.**

Examples include *4th rib, 8th month of pregnancy,* the *6th cranial nerve.* BOS recommends their usage be in numeric form and not spelled out.

- **Plurals and numbers.**

An apostrophe s ('s) is used to form a plural of a single-digit number, as in *4 x 4's.*

However, add an s without an apostrophe to pluralize multiple-digit numbers, as in: *30s, 1960s.*

- **Percentage and numbers.**

Use arabic numbers before the % sign when editing, as in *60%.* Do not place a space between the number and the % sign.

If a number begins the sentence, write out the number and write out percent, as in *Twelve percent of the patients were randomized in the study.*

If the amount is under 1%, then place a zero before the decimal, as in *0.4%* and not *.4%.*

If a range of values is given, repeat the % or the word percent with each value, as in

The lab values decreased from 59% to 40% in the last hour.

Four percent to eight percent of the patients had the flu.

Use decimals and not fractions when using percents, as in *0.5%* and not *½%.*

Be certain the subject and verb agree according to the wording. *Percent of* takes a singular verb when the word following *of* is singular. It takes a plural verb when the word following *of* is plural, as in:

Eighty percent of the eyelid was infected.

Fifteen percent of the patients were seen by the doctor on Wednesday.

When percent stands alone and is not followed by the word *of,* it takes on a singular verb, as in: *Six percent is inadequate.*

Review: Dangerous Abbreviations and Numbers

I. TRUE/FALSE.
Mark each of the following true or false according to Book of Style requirements.

1. The correct way to edit qhs is q.h.s.

   ○ true
   ○ false

2. An apostrophe s ('s) is used to form a plural of a single-digit number.

   ○ true
   ○ false

3. Arabic numerals are generally used when dealing with stages.

   ○ true
   ○ false

4. A colon is used to express suture size, as in 7:0 Vicryl.

   ○ true
   ○ false

5. The abbreviation AU might be mistaken for OU (each eye), so it is recommended not to use AU as an abbreviation when editing.

   ○ true
   ○ false

II. MULTIPLE CHOICE.
Determine the correct way to edit each of the following.

1. HCTZ

   ○ HCTZ
   ○ hydrochlorothiazide

2. From 10 to 20 percent.

   ○ From 10 to 20%
   ○ From 10% to 20%

3. The medication is to be taken q6pm.

   ○ The medication is to be taken 6 PM nightly
   ○ The medication is to be taken q.6pm.

4. The patient was born in the sixties.
   - ◯ The patient was born in the 60's
   - ◯ The patient was born in the 60s

5. She was given ten milligrams of saline.
   - ◯ She was given ten mg of saline
   - ◯ She was given 10 mg of saline

Lab Values and Headings

Laboratory Values and Data

Numbers are used to express lab values. There are some specifics to keep in mind within the guidelines being outlined here:

Commas are NOT to be used to separate lab values from the actual test. For example: *red blood cells 400* and not *red blood cells, 400.*

Multiple lab test results are to be separated by commas if they are related. Use semicolons if the series already has internal commas. For example: *Her pH was 7.4, specific gravity 1.025, and ketones were low.*

Unrelated tests get separated by periods.

When H and H is dictated, translate to hemoglobin and hematocrit for clarity.

Specific gravity is a value associated with urine and is expressed with four digits and a decimal point, as in:

Dictated: *The specific gravity was ten thirty.*

Edited: *The specific gravity was 1.030.*

Headings

There are acceptable variations in terms of how the headings and subheadings of a medical report are designed and set up; however, with regard to the formatting of those particular headings, BOS instructs that "institutional and client preferences should prevail." With this in mind, some variations in formatting headings and subheadings will be outlined in this section.

Some of the variations in capitalizing headings and subheadings are as follows:

LUNGS: Within normal limits.
or
Lungs: Within normal limits.
or
Lungs
Within normal limits.
or

LUNGS
Within normal limits.

In addition to the variations in capitalization, take note of the placement of the text that follows the heading as well as the colon usage. In every case, however, the first word following the heading or subheading is to be capitalized (in the above example, *Within normal limits*).

Book of Style has its own set of formatting preferences:

Capitals are to be used for all major section headings (i.e., LUNGS, CARDIOVASCULAR, etc.).

Initial capitals are to be used in subsection headings, as below:
HEENT
Eyes:
Ears:
Nose:

Each line of both headings and subheadings should end with a period unless it is the date or the name of a person as in:
SURGEON: Harold Jones, MD
SURGEON: Harold Jones, MD, and two others.

Headings that are not dictated but are obvious may be inserted and would be something contained within account specific instructions.

Abbreviations and brief forms of the words are not to be used in headings, unless the heading is commonly done this way, as in HEENT.

Most headings are to be listed vertically and without underlining, unless specified by the client.

One exception to capitalizing the first word after the heading or subheading pertains to quantity with unit of measure, as in estimated blood loss. In a case such as this, numerals are preferred as in:
ESTIMATED BLOOD LOSS: 5 mL.

I. **PROOFREADING.**
   Edit the following dictated statements to make them compliant with the BOS style.

   1. Dictated: The H and H were 12 and 36, respectively.

   2. Dictated: Cardiovascular: regular rate and rhythm.

   3. Dictated: Specific gravity was 1018.

   4. Dictated: His lab results revealed a ph of 7 point 1 and protein of 7 milligrams per deciliter.

   5. Dictated: heent

Contractions, Hyphens, Genus and Species

Contractions

Contractions should not be used unless they are a part of a direct quotation. In addition, abbreviations that contain contractions should be expanded. For example:

Dictated	Edited
won't	will not
he's	he is
it's	it is
OD'd	overdosed

Hyphenation

Both English and medical dictionaries should be consulted for proper hyphen use, but some general rules to remember follow:

Hyphens should be used to clarify meaning in certain words, such as *re-create* (to make again) instead of *recreate* (play) or *re-cover* (to cover again) and not *recover* (from an illness).

Use hyphens for pronunciation assistance as in: *co-workers* or *re-study*.

Use a hyphen when "numbers are used with words as compound modifiers preceding nouns." Examples of this are:

A 2-cm mass
The 10-mm cyst
A 6-cm incision

Suspensive hyphens are used to connect compound modifiers with the same base term as in:

The 2- and 3-mm growths
4- and 5-inch gauze

Use a hyphen when an adjective or participle is coupled with an adverb to form a compound modifier IF they precede the modifying noun but not if they follow it, as in:

A well-developed and well-nourished male patient.
versus
A male patient who is well developed and well nourished.

If an adverb ends in -ly, a hyphen should not be used when linking with a participle or adjective, as in *moderately severe pain* or *recently completed blood tests.*

The words high and low are usually hyphenated in most cases of compound adjectives, as in *low-frequency waves* or *high-density lesion.*

Numerals with words: If a number and a word form a compound modifier before a noun, it should be hyphenated as in: *2-week history* or *7-pound 3-ounce infant.*

For clarity, a hyphen is sometimes used, as in *small-bowel injury*, meaning an injury to the small bowel and not a small injury of the bowel.

Specialties: Some medical specialties, such as cardiology, use a hyphen when a term is used as an adjective, as in:

ST-T elevation
T-wave abnormality
Q-wave inversion

Genus and Species

The **genus** name is always capitalized when accompanied by the **species** name. In addition, abbreviated forms of the genus name are capitalized when accompanied by the species name. Examples are:

- Escherichia coli
- S. aureus

However, genus names should be in lowercase when used in the plural or adjectival form (or in the vernacular usage of the genus). Examples are:

- staphylococcus
- group B strep
- strep throat

I. **TRUE/FALSE.**
   The following are punctuated correctly: true or false?

   1. A 4 week history of pain.
      - ○ true
      - ○ false

   2. His large-bowel injury.
      - ○ true
      - ○ false

   3. The patient stated, "You won't be able to help me today."
      - ○ true
      - ○ false

   4. The doctor couldnt see the patient this afternoon.
      - ○ true
      - ○ false

   5. She is a young, well-appearing, healthy female.
      - ○ true
      - ○ false

   6. The patient is young, well-appearing, and healthy.
      - ○ true
      - ○ false

7. The patient was diagnosed with e. coli.

   ○ true
   ○ false

8. I asked my co-workers to come with me.

   ○ true
   ○ false

9. The lab results showed escherichia coli.

   ○ true
   ○ false

10. The EKG showed a Q-wave abnormality.

    ○ true
    ○ false

Answer Key

Patient Information

I. TRUE/FALSE.

1. true
2. false
3. false
4. true

Subjective/Objective Data

I. MULTIPLE CHOICE.

1. subjective
2. objective
3. objective
4. subjective

Documentation Standards

Healthcare Documentation Organizations

I. FILL IN THE BLANK.

1. American College of Surgeons
2. Utilization Review Accreditation Commission
3. American Health Information Management Association
4. College of American Pathologists
5. Accreditation Association for Ambulatory Healthcare
6. National Committee for Quality Assurance
7. Commission on Accreditation of Rehabilitation Facilities
8. American Medical Accreditation Program
9. American Osteopathic Association
10. American Accreditation Healthcare Commission

Consistency

CHALLENGE BOX.

1. **Qualitative analysis**
2. **Quantitative analysis**

Review: Consistency and Auditing

II. MATCHING.

1. G. Review of the medical record while the patient is still a patient.

2. H. Developed to ensure the uniformity, accuracy, and completeness of medical record entries.

3. A. Complete, legible, and chronological account of patient care.

4. I. Review of medical record to ensure that documentation standards are met.

5. C. Organization which accredits hospitals based on accreditation standards.

6. E. Review of the medical record to identify potential medical errors.

7. B. Incomplete or unclear information in a medical record.

8. D. Medical record review performed after the patient has been discharged.

9. F. Common definitions of medical terms in the patient's medical record.

10. J. Medical record review for completeness.

III. FILL IN THE BLANK.

1. documentation standards
2. acceptable documentation
3. concurrent review
4. occurrence screening
5. qualitative analysis
6. quantitative analysis
7. unacceptable documentation
8. retrospective review

Risk Management

I. FILL IN THE BLANK.

1. risk management
2. everyone
3. fraud and abuse
4. detection and prevention

Common Errors – Scenarios 1 and 2

I. MULTIPLE CHOICE.

1. patient name

II. MULTIPLE CHOICE.

1. gender inconsistency

Common Errors – Scenarios 3 and 4

I. MULTIPLE CHOICE.

1. date inconsistency

II. MULTIPLE CHOICE.

1. none of the above

Patient Confidentiality

EHR Challenges

I. MATCHING.

1. E. Standards developed to collect and transfer healthcare information between computer systems.
2. A. Record of a patient's health information which is created and stored in a computer.
3. C. Simultaneous access to a patient's health information to improve the quality of healthcare.
4. B. Privacy law which protects the confidentiality of electronically stored health information.
5. D. Medical record data printed and stored on paper.

II. TRUE/FALSE.

1. false
2. false
3. true
4. false
5. true

III. MULTIPLE CHOICE.

1. easy access for family and friends
2. all of the above
3. SNOMED
4. myocardial infarction
5. finding a place to store the electronic records

Health Insurance Portability and Accountability Act (HIPAA)

I. MULTIPLE CHOICE.

1. 1996
2. all of the above
3. existing laws were insufficient to deal with the threat technology posed to privacy
4. 2003

Internal Facility Policies

I. MATCHING.

1. D. access control
2. C. transfer of data
3. A. use of the internet
4. F. offsite work
5. E. storage of health information
6. B. audits

Review: HIPAA

I. MULTIPLE CHOICE.

1. all of the above
2. in 2003
3. Restore trust in the government.
4. Restrict healthcare provider's ability to file medical claims.
5. Leaving your work computer on when you take a break.
6. all of the above
7. Accessing the patient's medical record to code an operative report.
8. all of the above
9. The responsibility of employees.
10. a statement of the employee's legal and ethical guidelines

Consent to Release Medical Information

I. MULTIPLE CHOICE.

1. release of information form

2. when you want your sister, a nurse, to review your records

3. implied consent

4. if you contract a communicable disease and the Center for Disease Control needs to be notified

Medical Record Work Types

Medical Record Work Types – Introduction

I. TRUE/FALSE.

1. false
2. false
3. true
4. false
5. false
6. true
7. false
8. false
9. true
10. true

Report Components

Clinic Note Components

I. MULTIPLE CHOICE.

1. How the physician interprets the findings; an opinion, impression, assessment, or diagnosis

2. Treatment and followup, including medication regimen, instruction, suggested education, and followup instruction

3. A narrative of the patient's own description of his/her complaints: a past history, review of systems, allergies, or medication lists

4. The description of the physician's findings on observation and examination, any physical signs, and laboratory testing or diagnostic studies, such as x-rays

Standard Acute Care Components

I. FILL IN THE BLANK.

1. History
2. Social History
3. Hospital course
4. Review of Systems
5. Chief Complaint
6. Physical Examination
7. Past Medical History
8. Medications
9. Plan
10. Surgical History
11. Diagnosis/Assessment
12. Family History
13. Diagnostic Studies
14. Allergies

Operative Note Components

I. MATCHING.

1. B. Preoperative Diagnosis
3. D. Operations
5. F. Assistant Surgeon(s)
7. H. Estimated Blood Loss
9. J. Procedure

2. G. Postoperative Diagnosis
4. E. Surgeon
6. I. Anesthesia
8. C. Indication for Operation
10. A. Findings

Physical Examination

PE Abbreviations – Lesson 1

II. FILL IN THE BLANK.

1. clubbing, cyanosis, or edema OR cyanosis, clubbing, or edema
3. tympanic membranes

5. serous otitis media
7. blood pressure
9. central nervous system

2. Bartholin glands, urethra, and Skene glands
4. auscultation and percussion OR auscultation & percussion
6. regular rate and rhythm
8. arteriovenous
10. costovertebral angle

PE Abbreviations – Lesson 2

II. MATCHING.

1. A. HEENT
3. A. HEENT
5. A. HEENT

2. B. Neck
4. D. Neurological

PE Abbreviations – Lesson 3

II. FILL IN THE BLANK.

1. heart
3. joint
5. distress
7. eyes
9. left

2. normocephalic
4. right
6. delirium
8. jugular
10. ventricular

PE Abbreviations – Lesson 4

II. FILL IN THE BLANK.

1. right
3. round
5. range
7. maximal
9. upper

2. breath
4. amputation
6. rapid
8. above
10. lower

Physical Examination Samples

I. MULTIPLE CHOICE.

1. HEENT
3. clubbing, cyanosis, or edema
5. PERRLA

2. head, eyes, ears, nose, throat
4. genitourinary
6. RRR: regular rate and rhythm

Physical Examination Subheadings

I. TRUE/FALSE.

1. true
3. false

2. true
4. false

General and Vital Signs

I. MULTIPLE CHOICE.

1. hypotensive
3. state of alertness, personal hygiene, appearance, mood, etc.

2. cyanotic
4. Patient is 5 feet 6 inches, 175 pounds. Her blood pressure is 124/75.

HEENT

I. FILL IN THE BLANK.

1. Head
3. Eyes
5. Throat

2. Nose
4. Ears

Cardiovascular, Abdomen, and GU

I. MULTIPLE CHOICE.

1. fluid wave
3. perineal
5. Cardiovascular/Heart

2. heaves
4. Abdomen

Musculoskeletal

I. MULTIPLE CHOICE.

1. below-knee amputation
3. Palpation of the back reveals normal paraspinous muscle group with slight tenderness over C4.

2. muscles, bones, and joints of the body

Neurologic and Psychiatric

I. FILL IN THE BLANK.

1. nystagmus
3. neurologic

2. tangential
4. psychiatric

Review: Physical Examination Subheadings

I. SPELLING.

1. trachea midline
2. nontender
3. guaiac
4. clonus
5. carotid bruits
6. asymmetric
7. Romberg
8. posterior tibial
9. plantar
10. homicidal ideation

II. MULTIPLE CHOICE.

1. General
2. Neck
3. age
4. Musculoskeletal
5. eyes
6. Cardiovascular
7. Neck
8. HEENT
9. percussion
10. afebrile

Laboratory Data

Laboratory Abbreviations – Lesson 1

II. FILL IN THE BLANK.

1. dioxide
2. urea
3. count
4. arterial
5. sensitivity
6. bacillus

III. MULTIPLE CHOICE.

1. carbon
2. culture
3. arterial
4. count
5. urea

Laboratory Abbreviations – Lesson 2

II. FILL IN THE BLANK.

1. function
2. hemoglobin
3. immunodeficiency
4. cerebrospinal

III. MULTIPLE CHOICE.

1. hemoglobin
2. cerebrospinal
3. immunodeficiency
4. liver

Laboratory Abbreviations – Lesson 3

II. FILL IN THE BLANK.

1. prothrombin
2. thromboplastin
3. lumbar
4. ova
5. function
6. antigen

III. MULTIPLE CHOICE.

1. ova
2. function
3. partial
4. time
5. antigen

Laboratory Abbreviations – Lesson 4

II. FILL IN THE BLANK.

1. blood
2. tuberculosis
3. cells
4. urinalysis

III. MULTIPLE CHOICE.

1. urinalysis
2. red
3. white
4. tuberculosis

Basic Laboratory Studies – Lesson 1

I. MULTIPLE CHOICE.

1. hemoglobin and platelets
2. Beta HCG
3. ABG
4. Cardiac Studies
5. the time it takes for blood to clot
6. CMP
7. LP (lumbar puncture)
8. sodium, potassium, BUN, glucose, and calcium

Basic Laboratory Studies – Lesson 2

I. MULTIPLE CHOICE.

1. endocrine panel
2. PSA
3. SMA
4. serum iron
5. Lipid profile
6. Renal function tests
7. BUN
8. TIBC, ferritin, and transferrin
9. Urinalysis
10. lytes
11. Hepatic function tests

Review: Laboratory Studies

I. MULTIPLE CHOICE.

1. sodium
2. TIBC
3. CBC
4. coagulation
5. drugs
6. overactive
7. SGOT/SGPT
8. blood urea nitrogen

II. TRUE/FALSE.

1. false
2. true
3. false
4. true

Lab Reports – Lesson 1

I. SPELLING.

1. sodium
2. bicarbonate
3. protein
4. hemoglobin
5. hematocrit
6. potassium
7. specific gravity
8. urinalysis
9. BUN
10. platelets

Lab Reports – Lesson 2

I. MULTIPLE CHOICE.
1. corpuscular
2. dioxide
3. urea
4. prothrombin
5. thromboplastin

Lab Reports – Lesson 3

I. MATCHING.
1. C. occult
2. F. glucose
3. G. electrolyte
4. A. atelectasis
5. E. creatinine
6. B. macrocytosis
7. D. platelets
8. H. white blood cells

Review: Normal Laboratory Values

I. MULTIPLE CHOICE.
1. hemoglobin
2. creatinine
3. hemoglobin 13
4. 37.2
5. hyperglycemic

II. TRUE/FALSE.
1. false
2. true
3. true
4. false
5. true

Formatting

General Formatting Rules

I. TRUE/FALSE.
1. false
2. true
3. false
4. false
5. true

Abbreviations and Brief Forms

I. MULTIPLE CHOICE.
1. CABG
2. by mouth
3. A grouping of initials that you would NOT say aloud as you would an acronym.
4. brief form
5. b.i.d.

II. MATCHING.
1. C. n.r.
2. B. u.d.
3. E. p.c.
4. A. q.h.
5. D. gtt.

Slang

I. MULTIPLE CHOICE.

1. micrograms
2. perf
3. Alzheimer
4. potassium chloride
5. differential
6. bundle of His
7. appy
8. dipyridamole sestamibi
9. eponym
10. sat

Foreign Terms

I. SPELLING.

1. mittelschmerz
2. peau d'orange
3. cerclage
4. sitz
5. en masse
6. coup
7. steinstrasse
8. raphe
9. ad libitum
10. lavage
11. cafe au lait spot
12. grand mal
13. statim
14. en bloc
15. status quo

Review: Dangerous Abbreviations and Numbers

I. TRUE/FALSE.

1. false
2. true
3. false
4. false
5. true

II. MULTIPLE CHOICE.

1. hydrochlorothiazide
2. From 10% to 20%
3. The medication is to be taken 6 PM nightly
4. The patient was born in the 60s
5. She was given 10 mg of saline

Lab Values and Headings

I. PROOFREADING.

1. The ~~H~~ **hemoglobin** and ~~H~~ **hematocrit** were 12 and 36, respectively.
2. ~~Cardiovascular~~ **CARDIOVASCULAR**: ~~regular~~ **Regular** rate and rhythm.
3. Specific gravity was ~~1018~~ **1.018**.
4. His lab results revealed a ~~ph~~ **pH** of ~~7 point 1~~ **7.1** and protein of 7 ~~milligrams per deciliter~~ **mg/dL**.
5. ~~heent~~ **HEENT**

Contractions, Hyphens, Genus and Species

I. TRUE/FALSE.

1. false
2. true
3. true
4. false
5. true
6. false
7. false
8. true
9. false
10. true

Appendix

PATIENT HISTORY

NAME: LAST	FIRST		MIDDLE	DOB		AGE	SEX
							M ___ F

EMERGENCY CONTACT PERSON			RELATIONSHIP		HOME PHONE: ( )
PHARMACY PHONE #:	HEIGHT	WEIGHT	OCCUPATION		

CURRENT MEDICAL PROBLEMS

IF YOU ARE BEING TREATED FOR ANY OTHER ILLNESSES OR MEDICAL PROBLEMS BY ANOTHER PHYSICIAN, PLEASE DESCRIBE THE PROBLEMS & INDICATE THE NAME OF THE PHYSICIAN TREATING YOU.

ILLNESS OR MEDICAL PROBLEMS	PHYSICIANS TREATING YOU

ILLNESS AND MEDICAL PROBLEMS

PLEASE MARK WITH A (X) ANY OF THE FOLLOWING ILLNESSES & MEDICAL PROBLEMS YOU HAVE OR HAVE HAD. ALSO INDICATE THE YEAR WHEN EACH STARTED. IF YOU ARE NOT CERTAIN WHEN THE ILLNESS STARTED, WRITE DOWN AN APPROXIMATE YEAR.

ILLNESS	X	YEAR	ILLNESS	X	YEAR	ILLNESS	X	YEAR
MIGRAINE HEADACHES			HIGH BLOOD PRESSURE			JAUNDICE		
HEADACHES			HEART ATTACK			LIVER TROUBLE		
HEAD INJURY			HIGH CHOLESTEROL			GALLBLADDER PROBLEMS		
STROKE			POOR CIRCULATION			HERNIA		
SEIZURE			HEART MURMUR			HEMORRHOIDS		
GLAUCOMA			BLEEDING TENDENCY			KIDNEY DISEASE		
OTHER EYE PROBLEMS			ANEMIA			BLADDER DISEASE		
DEAFNESS			OTHER HEART COND.			PROSTATE PROBLEMS		
BRONCHITIS			BREAST CANCER			KIDNEY STONES		
EMPHYSEMA			COLON CANCER			ARTHRITIS		
PNEUMONIA			PROSTATE CANCER			CHICKEN POX		
ALLERGIES			OTHER CANCER			DIABETES		
ASTHMA			ULCER			HEPATITIS		
TUBERCULOSIS			DIVERTICULITIS			MEASLES		
MENTAL ILLNESS			SUBSTANCE ABUSE			PSORIASIS		

160

ALCOHOLISM			AIDS/HIV			VENEREAL DISEASE		
THYROID DISEASE			RHEUMATIC FEVER					

IMMUNIZATIONS

DATE OF LAST TETANUS SHOT	INFLUENZA VACCINE	GERMAN MEASLES VACCINE

MEDICATIONS

PLEASE LIST ALL MEDICATIONS YOU ARE NOW TAKING, INCLUDING THOSE YOU TAKE WITHOUT A DOCTOR'S PRESCRIPTION (SUCH AS ASPIRIN OR COLD TABLETS).

1.	2.	3.
4.	5.	6.
7.	8.	9.
10.	11.	12.
13.	14.	15.

ALLERGIES AND SENSITIVITIES

LIST ANYTHING THAT YOU ARE ALLERGIC TO, SUCH AS CERTAIN FOODS, MEDICATIONS, DUST, CHEMICALS OR SOAPS, HOUSEHOLD ITEMS, POLLEN, BEE STINGS, ETC. INDICATE HOW EACH AFFECTS YOU.

ALLERGIC TO:	REACTION:	ALLERGIC TO:	REACTION:
1.		5.	
2.		6.	
3.		7.	
4.		8.	

SOCIAL/PERSONAL HISTORY

DO YOU SMOKE? ___YES ___NO   IF YES, HOW MANY PACKS PER DAY? _____
ARE YOU A FORMER SMOKER? ___YES ___NO   IF YES HOW MANY MONTHS/YEARS SINCE YOU QUIT?

DO YOU DRINK ALCOHOLIC BEVERAGES? ___YES ___NO   HOW MANY OUNCES PER DAY? _____
IF YES WHAT TYPE OF ALCOHOL, (I.E. BEER, WINE, LIQUOR)?
_____

HOW MANY BEERS DO YOU DRINK PER DAY? _____

DO YOU DRINK COLA, COFFEE OR TEA? ___YES ___NO	DO YOU WEAR A SEAT BELT? ___YES ___NO DO YOU WEAR SUNBLOCK? ___YES ___NO

DO YOU USE RECREATIONAL DRUGS/NOT PURCHASED AT A DRUG STORE?   ___YES ___NO

ARE THERE ANY RELIGIOUS OR CULTURE ISSUES THAT MAY AFFECT YOUR MEDICAL CARE?

FAMILY HISTORY

RELATIONSHIP:	AGE IF LIVING	AGE AT DEATH	STATE OF HEALTH OR CAUSE OF DEATH	ILLNESS	FATHER	MOTHER	BROTHER	SISTER
FATHER				HEART DISEASE				
MOTHER				HIGH BLOOD PRESSURE				
BROTHER (S)				CANCER				
SISTER (S)				DIABETES				
SPOUSE				BLOOD DISEASE				
				EPILEPSY				
				RHEUMATOID ARTHRITIS				
CHILDREN				GOUT				
				GLAUCOMA				
				TUBERCULOSIS				

PLEASE GIVE THE FOLLOWING INFORMATION ABOUT YOUR IMMEDIATE FAMILY:

HAVE ANY BLOOD RELATIVES HAD ANY OF THE FOLLOWING ILLNESSES? IF SO, INDICATE RELATIONSHIP BY PLACING AN "X" IN THE APPROPRIATE BOX:

MEN ONLY – ANY PROBLEMS WITH THE FOLLOWING

HERNIA ___ YES ___ NO	PAIN IN TESTICLES ___ YES ___ NO	SEXUAL DIFFIC. ___ YES ___ NO
DISCHARGE FROM PENIS ___ YES ___ NO	SEXUALLY TRANSMITTED DISEASE ___ YES ___ NO	

WOMEN ONLY – ANY PROBLEMS WITH THE FOLLOWING

VAGINAL ITCHING/BURNING _____
VAGINAL DISCHARGE _____
PROBLEM WITH MENSTRUAL PERIODS _____
FIRST MENSTRUAL PERIOD _____
DATE OF LAST MENSTRUAL PERIOD _____
DATE OF LAST PAP SMEAR _____
METHOD OF CONTRACEPTION _____
SEXUALLY TRANSMITTED DISEASE _____

SEXUAL DIFFICULTIES _____
NUMBER OF PREGNANCIES _____
NUMBER OF MISCARRIAGES/ABORTIONS _____
NUMBER OF LIVE BIRTHS _____
PROBLEMS WITH PREGNANCIES _____
LUMPS IN BREAST _____
DISCHARGE FROM NIPPLE(S) _____
DATE OF LAST MAMMOGRAM _____

DID YOU MISS MORE THAN (10) DAYS OF YOUR USUAL ACTIVITY LAST YEAR DUE TO ILLNESS OR INJURY? IF YES, PLEASE EXPLAIN:

_____
_____
_____

_____   _____
PATIENT SIGNATURE   DATE   PHYSICIAN INITALS/DATE

NOTICE OF PRIVACY PRACTICES

THIS NOTICE DESCRIBES HOW MEDICAL INFORMATION ABOUT YOU MAY BE USED AND DISCLOSED AND HOW YOU CAN GET ACCESS TO THIS INFORMATION. PLEASE REVIEW CAREFULLY.

This Notice of Privacy Practices is being provided to you as a requirement of the Health Insurance Portability and Accountability Act (HIPAA). This Notice describes how we may use and disclose your Protected Health Information (PHI) to carry out treatment, payment or health care operation and for other purposes that are permitted or required by law. It also describes your rights to access and control your Protected Health Information in **some cases.** Your "Protected Health Information" means any of your written and oral health information, including demographic data that can identify you. This health information is created or received by our office (your health care provider) and/or other physicians whose care you are under, and that relates to your past, present or future physical or mental health condition.

I. Uses and Disclosures of Protected Health Information

The practice may use your protected health information for purposes of providing treatment, obtaining payment for treatment and conducting health care operations. Your protected health care information my be used or disclosed only for these purposes unless _____ [Organization Name] has obtained your authorization or the use or disclosure is other wise permitted by the HIPAA Privacy Regulations or State Law. Disclosures of your protected health information for the purposes described in this Notice may be made in writing, orally or by facsimile.

A.   **Treatment:** We will use and disclose your protected health information to provide, coordinate, or manage your health care and any related services. This includes the coordination or management of your health care with a third party for treatment purposes. For example, we may disclose your protected health information to a pharmacy to fulfill a prescription, to a laboratory to order a blood test, or to a home health care agency that is providing care in your home. We may also disclose protected health information to other physicians who may be treating you or consulting with your physician with respect to your care. In some cases, we may also disclose your protected health information to an outside treatment provider for purposes of the treatment activities of the other provider.

B.   **Payment:** Your protected health information will be used, as needed, to obtain payment for the services that we provide. This may include certain communications to your health insurer to obtain approval for the treatment that we recommend. For example, if a hospital admission is recommended, we may need to disclose information to your health insurer to obtain prior approval for the hospitalization. We may also disclose protected health information to your insurance company to determine whether you are eligible for benefits or whether a particular service is covered under your health plan. In order to obtain payment for your services, we may also need to disclose your protected health information to your insurance carrier to demonstrate the medical necessity of the services or, as required by your insurance company, for utilization review. We may also disclose patient information to another provider involved in your care for the other provider's payment activities.

C.   **Operations:** We may use or disclose your protected health information, as necessary, for our own health care operations and to provide quality of care to our patients. Health care operations include such activities as:

- Quality assessment and improvement activities
- Employee review activities
- Training programs including those in which students, trainees, or practitioners in health care learn under supervision
- Accreditation, certification, licensing or credentialing activities
- Review and auditing, including compliance review, medical reviews, legal reviews and maintaining compliance programs.
- Business management and general administrative activities.

In certain situations, we may also disclose patient information to another provider or health plan for their health care operations.

D.   **Other Uses and Disclosures:** As part of treatment, payment and healthcare operations, we may also use or disclose your protected health information for the following purposes:

- To remind you of your appointment
- To inform you of potential treatment alternative or options
- To inform you of health-related benefits or services that may be of interest to you.

II. Uses and Disclosures Beyond Treatment, Payment and Health Care Operations Permitted without Authorization or Opportunity to Object

Federal privacy rules allow us to use or disclose your protected health information without your permission or authorization for a number of reasons including the following:

A. **When Legally Required:** We will disclose your protected health information when we are required to do so by any Federal, State or Local law.

B. **When There Are Risks to Public Health:** We may disclose your protected health information for the following public activities and purposes:

- To prevent, control or report disease, injury or disability as permitted by law.
- To report vital events such as birth or death as permitted or required by law.
- To conduct public health surveillance, investigations and interventions as permitted or required by law.
- To collect or report adverse events and product defects, track FDA regulated products, enable product recalls, repairs or replacements to the FDA and to conduct post marketing surveillance.
- To notify a person who has been exposed to a communicable disease or who may be at risk of contracting or spreading a disease as authorized by law.
- To report to an employer information about an individual who is a member of the workforce as legally permitted or required by law.

C. **To Report Abuse, Neglect Or Domestic Violence:** We may notify government authorities if we believe that a patient is the victim of abuse, neglect or domestic violence. We will make this disclosure only when specifically required or authorized by law or when the patient agrees to the disclosure.

D. **To Conduct Health Oversight Activities:** We may disclose your protected health information to a health oversight agency for activities including audits; civil, administrative, or criminal investigations, proceedings, or actions; inspections; licensure or disciplinary actions; or other activities necessary for appropriate oversight as authorized by law. We will not disclose your health information if you are the subject of an investigation and your health information is not directly related to your receipt of health care or public benefits.

E. **In Connection with Judicial and Administrative Proceedings:** We may disclose your protected health information in the course of any judicial or administrative proceeding in response to an order of a court or administrative tribunal as expressly authorized by such order or in response to a signed authorization.

165

F.   **For Law Enforcement Purposes:** We may disclose your protected health information to law enforcement official for law enforcement purposes as follows:

- As required by law for reporting of certain types of wounds or other physical injuries.
- Pursuant to court order, court-ordered warrant, subpoena or summons.
- For the purpose of identifying or locating a suspect, or missing person.
- Under certain limited circumstances, when you are a victim of a crime.
- To a law enforcement official if the practice has a suspicion that your death was the result of a criminal conduct.
- In an emergency in order to report a crime.

G.   **To Coroners, Funeral Directors and for Organ Donation:** We may disclose protected health information to a coroner or medical examiner for identification purposes, to determine cause of death or for the coroner or medical examiner to perform other duties authorized by law. We may also disclose protected health information to a funeral director, as authorized by law, in order to permit the funeral director to carry out their duties. We may disclose such information in reasonable anticipation of death. Protected health information may be used and disclosed for cadaveric organ, eye or tissue donation purposes.

H.   **For Research Purposes:** We may use or disclose your protected health information for research when the use or disclosure for research has been approved by an institutional review board or privacy board that has reviewed the research proposal and research protocols to address the privacy of your protected health information.

I.   **In the Event of A Serious Threat to Health Or Safety:** We may, consistent with applicable law and ethical standards of conduct use or disclose your protected health information if we believe, in good faith, that such use or disclosure is necessary to prevent or lessen a serious and imminent threat to your health or safety or to the health and safety of the public.

J.   **For Specified Government Functions:** In certain circumstances, the federal regulations authorize the practice to use or disclose your protected health information to facilitate specified government functions relating to military and veteran activities, national security, and intelligence activities, protective services for the President and others, medical suitability determinations, correctional institutions, and law enforcement custodial situations.

K.   **For Worker's Compensation:** The practice may release your protected health information to comply with worker's compensation laws.

III   **Uses and Disclosures Permitted Without Authorization But With Opportunity to Object:**

We may disclose your protected health information to your family member or a close personal friend if it is directly relevant to the person's involvement in your care or payment related to your care. We can also disclose your information in connection with trying to locate or notify family members or others involved in your care concerning your location, condition or death.

You may object to these disclosures. If you do not object to these disclosures or we can infer from circumstances that you do not object or we determine, in the exercise of our professional judgment, which it is in your best interests for us to make disclosure of information that is directly relevant to the person's involvement with your care, we may disclose your protected health information as described.

IV   **Uses and Disclosures Which You Can Authorize:**

Other than as stated above, we will not disclose your protected health Information other than with your written authorization. You may revoke your Authorization in writing at any time except to the extent that we have taken action In reliance upon the authorization.

V   **Your Rights:**

You have the following rights regarding your health information:

A. **The right to inspect and copy our protected health information:** You may inspect and obtain a copy of your protected health information that is contained in a designated record set for as long as we maintain the protected health information. A "designated record set" contains medical and billing records and any other records that your physician and the practice use for making decisions about you.

Under Federal law, however, you may not inspect or copy the following records:

- Psychotherapy Notes
- Information compiled in reasonable anticipation of or for use in a civil, criminal or administrative action or proceeding
- Protected health information that is subject to a law prohibits access to protected health information.

Depending on the circumstances, you may have the right to have a decision to deny access reviewed.

We may deny your request to inspect or copy your protected health information if, in our professional judgment, we determine that the access requested is likely to endanger your life or safety or that of another person, or that it is likely to cause substantial harm to another person, or that it is likely to cause substantial harm to another person referenced within the information. You have the right to request a review of this decision.

To inspect and copy your medical information, you must submit a written request to the Privacy Officer whose contact information is listed on the last pages of this Notice. If you request a copy of your information, we will charge you a fee for the cost of copying, mailing and other costs incurred by use in complying with your request.

Please contact the Privacy Officer if you have questions about access to your medical record.

B. **The right to request a restriction on uses and disclosures of your Protected Health information:**

You may ask us not to use or disclose certain parts of your protected health information for the purposes of treatment, payment or health care operations. You may also request that we not disclose your health information to family members or friends who may be involved in your care or for notification purposes as described in this Notice of Privacy Practices. Your request must state the specific restriction requested to whom you want the restrictions apply.

The practice is not required to agree to a restriction that you may request. We will notify you if we deny your request to a restriction. If the practice does agree to the requested restriction, we may not use or disclose your protected health information in violation of that restriction unless it is needed to provide emergency treatment. Under certain circumstances, we may terminate our agreement to a restriction. You may request a restriction by contacting the Privacy Officer.

C. **The right to request to receive confidential communication from us by alternative means or at an alternative location.**

You have the right to request that we communicate with you in certain ways. We will accommodate reasonable requests. We may condition this accommodation by asking you for information as to how payment will be handled or specifications of alternative address or other method of contact. We will require you to provide an explanation for your request. Request must be made in writing to the Privacy Officer.

D. **The right to have your physician amend your protected health information:**

You may request an amendment of protected health information about your in a designated record set for as long as we maintain this information. In certain cases, we may deny your request for an amendment. If we deny your request for amendment, you have the right to file a statement of disagreement with us and we may prepare a rebuttal to your statement and will provide you with a copy of any such rebuttal. Request for amendment must be in writing and must be direct to our Privacy Officer. In this written Request, you must also provide a reason to support the requested amendments.

E.   <u>The right to receive an accounting:</u>

You have the right to request an account of certain disclosures of your protected health information made by the practice. This right applies to disclosures for purposes other than treatment, payment, health care operations as described in this Notice of Privacy Practices. We are also not required to account for disclosures that you requested, disclosures that you agreed to by signing an authorization form, disclosures for a facility directory, to friends or family members involved in your care or certain other disclosure we are permitted to make without your authorization. The request for an accounting must be made in writing to our Privacy Officer. The request should specify the time period sought for the accounting.

Accounting request may not be made for periods of time in excess of six year. We will Provide for the first account you request during any12 month period without charge. Subsequent request will be subject to a reasonable cost-based fee.

F.   <u>The right to obtain a copy of this Notice:</u>

You will need to sign a copy of this Notice which will be filed in your chart. You may also request a copy of this Notice for your own records.

VI.   <u>Our Duties:</u>

The practice is required by law to maintain the privacy of your protected health information and to provide you with this Notice of our duties and privacy practices. We are required to abide by terms of this Notice as may be amended from time to time. We reserve the right to change the terms of this Notice and to make the new Notice provisions effective for all protective health information that we maintain. If the practice changes its Notice, we will provide a copy of the revised Notice through an in person contact or via regular mail at your request.

VII.   <u>Complaints:</u>

You have the right express complaint to the practice and to the Secretary of Health and Human Services if you believe that your privacy rights have been violated. You may complain to the practice by contacting the practice's Privacy Officer in writing, using the Contact information below. We encourage you to express any concerns you may have regarding the privacy of your information. You will not be retaliated against in any way for filing a complaint.

VIII. **Contact Person:**

The practice's contact person for all issues regarding patient privacy and your rights under the Federal privacy standards is the Privacy Officer. Information regarding matters covered in this Notice can be request by contacting the Privacy Officer. Complaints against the practice, can be mailed to the Privacy Officer at:

XYZ Physician's
Attention: Privacy Officer
123 Maple Street
Anywhere, USA 12345

Indicate on the envelope - **Personal & Confidential**

IX. **Effective Date: January 12, 2006**

I have read and understand the Notice of Privacy Practices given to me:

_____

Patient Name (Printed) & Signature   Date

ACKNOWLEDGMENT OF RECEIPT OF NOTICE OF PRIVACY PRACTICES

I acknowledge that I have received or been offered the Notice of Privacy Practices of _____ [Organization Name]. I understand that the Notice describes the uses and disclosures of my protected health information by _____ [Organization Name] and that they will inform me of my rights with respect to my protected health information.

_____

Name of Patient

_____   _____

Medical Record Number   Date of Birth

_____

Signature of Patient or Personal Representative

_____

Printed Name of Patient or Personal Representative

_____

Date

Declinations

_____   The Individual declined to accept a copy of the Notice of
Privacy Practices.

_____   The Individual received a copy of the Notice of Privacy
Practices but declined to sign an Acknowledgment of receipt.

_____   _____

Healthcare Representative Signature   Healthcare Representative Name

Confidentiality of Patient, Employee and Business Information
Statement of Policy

It is the legal and ethical responsibility of all employees, house staff, and volunteers to use personal and confidential patient, employee and business information (referred to here collectively as "confidential information") in accordance with the law and [Employer] policy, and to preserve and protect the privacy rights of the subject of the information as they perform their duties.

Laws controlling the privacy of, access to and maintenance of confidential information include, but are not limited to, the federal Health Insurance Portability and Accountability Act (HIPAA), the California Information Practices Act (IPA), the California Confidentiality of Medical Information Act (COMIA), and the Lanterman-Petris-Short Act (LPS). These and other laws apply whether the information is held in electronic or any other form, and whether the information is used or disclosed orally or in writing.

Confidential information includes information that identifies or describes an individual and the disclosure of which would constitute an unwarranted invasion of personal privacy. Examples of confidential employee and information include home address and telephone number; medical information; birth date; citizenship; social security number; spouse/partner/relative's names.

The term "medical information" includes the following: medical and psychiatric records, including paper printouts, photos, videotapes, diagnostic and therapeutic reports, x-rays, scans, laboratory and pathology samples; patient business records, such as bills for service or insurance information whether stored externally or on campus; electronically stored or transmitted patient information; visual observation of patients receiving medical care or accessing services; verbal information provide by or about a patient; peer review/risk management information and activities; or other information the disclosure of which would constitute an unwarranted invasion of privacy.

Acknowledgement of Responsibility
I understand and acknowledge that:

It is my legal and ethical responsibility to preserve and protect the privacy, confidentiality and security of all medical records, proprietary and other confidential information relating to [Employer], its patients, activities and affiliates, in accordance with the law and [Employer] policy.

I agree to access, use or disclose confidential information only in the performance of my duties, where required by or permitted by law, and only to persons who have the right to receive that information. When using or disclosing confidential information, I will use or disclose only the minimum information necessary.

I agree to discuss confidential information only in my workplace and for [Employer]-related purposes. I will not knowingly discuss any confidential information within the hearing of other persons who do not have the right to receive the information. I agree to protect the confidentiality of any medical, proprietary or other confidential information which is incidentally disclosed to me in the course of my relationship with [Employer].

I understand that psychiatric records, drug abuse records, and any and all references to HIV testing, such as clinical tests, laboratory or otherwise, used to identify HIV, a component of HIV, or antibodies or antigens to HIV, are specially protected by law.

I understand that my access to all [Employer] electronic information systems is subject to audit in accordance with [Employer] policy.

I agree not to share my Login or User ID and/or password with anyone and that any access to [Employer] electronic information systems made using my Login or User ID and password is my responsibility. If I believe someone else has used my Login or User ID and/or password, I will immediately report the use to internal information technology services and request a new password.

I understand that violation of any of the policies and procedures related to confidential information or of any state or federal laws or regulations governing a patient's right to privacy may subject me to legal and/or disciplinary action up to and including immediate termination from my employment/professional relationship with [Employer].

I understand that I may be personally liable for harm resulting from my breach of this Agreement and that I may also be held criminally liable under the HIPAA privacy regulations for an intentional and/or malicious release of protected health information.

_____   _____
Signature   Date

_____   _____
Print Name   Witness

PATIENT CONFIDENTIALITY ACKNOWLEDGMENT STATEMENT

I, _____, acknowledge that I have received a copy of Policy Statement entitled: Confidentiality of Patient Information. I have read the policy statement and understand its contents and how it applies to my position. I understand that breach of this policy may lead to disciplinary action, up to and including dismissal. I also understand that I am to ask my supervisor if at any time I have questions concerning patient confidentiality.

Employee's signature:

_____ Date signed: _____

Confidentiality Statement

As a user of information at [Employer] Healthcare System you may develop, us, or maintain

(1) Patient information (for healthcare, quality improvement, peer review, education, billing, reimbursement, administration, research or for other approved purposes),
(2) Personnel information (for employment, payroll, or other business purposes), or
(3) Confidential business information of [Employer] Healthcare System and/or third parties, including third-party software and other licensed products or processes. This information from any source and in any form, including, but not limited to, paper record, oral communication, audio recording, and electronic display, is strictly confidential. Access to confidential information is permitted only on a need-to-know basis and limited to the minimum amount of confidential information necessary to accomplish the intended purpose of the use, disclosure or request.

It is the policy of [Employer] Healthcare System that users (i.e., employees, medical staff, students, volunteers, vendors and other outside affiliates) shall respect and preserve the privacy, confidentiality and security of confidential information. **Violations of this statement include, but are not limited do:**

- **accessing confidential information that is not within the scope of your duties**
- **misusing, disclosing without proper authorization, or altering confidential information**
- **disclosing to another person your sign-on code and/or password for accessing electronic confidential information or for physical access to restricted areas**
- **using another person's sign-on code and/or password for accessing electronic confidential information or for physical access to restricted areas**
- **intentional or negligent mishandling or destruction of confidential information**
- **leaving a secured application unattended while signed on**
- **attempting to access a secured application or restricted area without proper authorization or for purposes other than official [Employer] Healthcare System business.**

Violation of this statement may constitute grounds for corrective action up to and including termination of employment, loss of [Employer] Healthcare System privileges or contractual or affiliation rights in accordance with applicable [Employer] Healthcare System procedures. Unauthorized use or release of confidential information may also subject the violator to personal, civil, and/or criminal liability and legal penalties.